THR _

Pam is such an engaging and encouraging advocate for the local church. This accessible, practical book is the fruit of deep thinking and much experience: it will be an invaluable guide towards growth for all engaged in multi-parish ministry.
Rt Revd Dr Andrew Rumsey, Bishop of Ramsbury, Diocese of Salisbury

Pam has worked with leaders of multi-parish benefices to enable their churches to flourish and thrive. The wisdom she has gleaned will be gold dust for MPBs and for all leaders in local churches.
Stephen Hance, Vision and Strategy team, Church of England

'Thrive' was such a source of encouragement and inspiration to our multi-parish benefice, enabling us to accept the realities of faith in the twenty-first century. Over the period of working with the 'Explore, plan, act and review' model we found ourselves equipped to face the challenge of past, present and future changes and encourage our people to grow into welcoming, nurturing communities. Looking back it seemed impossible that we could achieve the transitions we hoped for, but every one has borne fruit.
Bridget Gillespie, Thrive course participant

Churches in multi-parish benefices have huge potential to work together to serve their communities. Yet they often face unique and complex issues, meaning it can be a challenge to realize the potential for growth. The Thrive suite of resources are designed to help multi-parish benefices discover where their strengths lie, reflect on how to harness opportunities, and so unlock their potential to thrive as the gospel is shared anew. Pam Macnaughton's helpful and practical book shows what is possible and is a source of great encouragement rooted in her own experience as a church leader.
The Most Revd Stephen Cottrell, Archbishop of York

This book will be a gift to many multi-parish benefices. It reflects the challenges they face yet is hopeful about the incredible potential they represent. *Thrive – helping your MPB to grow* takes church leaders step by step on a practical, accessible and encouraging journey. It is based on years of experience, and it is hoped that the Thrive process will help the worshipping communities across multi-parish benefices to worship, reflect and reimagine, that we might continue to discover yet more of what it means to be the Church in and among our local communities.
The Rt Revd Rachel Treweek, Bishop of Gloucester

THRIVE

Helping Your
Multi-Parish Benefice
to Grow

Pam Macnaughton

CHURCH HOUSE
PUBLISHING

⊕ CHURCH HOUSE PUBLISHING

Church House Publishing	Church Pastoral Aid Society
Church House	Sovereign Court One (Unit 3)
Great Smith Street	Sir William Lyons Road
London SW1P 3AZ	University of Warwick Science Park
chpublishing.co.uk	Coventry CV4 7EZ
	www.cpas.org.uk

ISBN 978-1-78140-432-4

Published in 2023 by Church House Publishing.

Written by Pam Macnaughton. Edited by Di Archer.

Church Pastoral Aid Society
Registered charity 1007820 (England and Wales); registered charity
SC039082 (Scotland). A company limited by guarantee. Registered in
England 2673220. Registered office at above address.

The opinions expressed in this book are those of the author and do
not necessarily reflect the official policy of the General Synod or The
Archbishops' Council of the Church of England.

Printed and bound in England by
Ashford Colour Press Ltd.

Contents

For George and Cynthia.
Thank you for teaching me,
in your different ways,
how to pray.

Acknowledgements

I am so grateful to all who have cheered me on in the task of getting what I have learned over the last nine years into this book.

Specifically, I want to thank John Barton, Mat Ineson, Matt Hogg, Ruth Walker and Lesley Bentley, who all read and commented so insightfully on the first draft, and my colleague Charles Burgess, conversation and training partner for so much work with MPBs.

My boss at CPAS, James Lawrence, inspired me to tackle writing, to keep going and to sharpen the text. I am privileged to have worked with him, learned from him and had his oversight and help on this project.

My editor at CPAS, Diana Archer, has lived all the challenges of creation and deadlines with me and has worked with much grace, wisdom and persistence in shaping the book.

I could not have managed without any of these people. The remaining weaknesses and omissions in this book are, of course, my own.

Finally, so much thanks to my husband Malcolm, from whom many of the best ideas of leading MPBs over the years have come, and who has stood by me patiently and encouragingly on this writing journey.

About the Author

Pam Macnaughton has worked both as a lay leader and later an ordained pioneer associate minister in three different multi-parish benefices (MPBs) – in rural Buckinghamshire, suburban Yorkshire and now small-town Derbyshire. She has:

- planted new worshipping communities in two of those places;
- absorbed many stories of the realities of MPB life from lay and ordained leaders;
- kept abreast of the national picture through her role with CPAS;
- trained people of all ages in leadership and mission;
- developed a significant passion for the struggles of many church situations and a deep-rooted determination to help where possible;
- carried lifelong biases towards mission and younger generations;
- and clocked up many years' experience in writing and editing resources for churches.

She has run Thrive learning communities for multi-parish benefices for eight years across a number of dioceses, and watched them transform for the better, at the time and on into the future.

Pam currently works as a Churches and Networks Advisor for the Church of England Vision and Strategy Team.

Introduction – Start here

There was a palpable sense of relief in the room. It was growing as time progressed. In the discussion, there were 'Oh, it's not just us' comments. What was going on?

Ten years ago, I started developing and running learning-and-action communities for lay and ordained people in multi-parish benefices (MPBs) as part of the work of CPAS (Church Pastoral Aid Society, www.cpas.org.uk). Working across a diocese, incumbents were invited to collect a team of willing and committed people from their churches – some who were leaders, some who were not, and definitely a mix of lay and ordained. With around six of these teams, we spent two to three years journeying together. Through the combination of regular input and encouragement, practical planning, lots of prayer and hard work, I have seen MPBs transformed for the better.

However, back to that sense of relief. It occurred without fail every time during the first session when people realized they were not the only ones struggling with the joys and complexities of living and working in a group of churches, sharing clergy and lay leaders.

As they journeyed together, the relief turned into deeper hope, new vision and positive action. The MPB teams prayed for each other, supported each other, learned together and took on and adapted each other's ideas and experiences. They shared their plans with each other at the end of each gathering and reported back on them every six months. This built-in accountability kept them focused and active.

In these learning-and-action communities, I have seen groups start new initiatives and plant new congregations. I have seen them deepen their prayer lives and encourage new disciples. I have seen lay and ordained leaders get to know each other across an MPB and learn to work together creatively, prayerfully and effectively. I have seen them grow new leaders and launch out into work with children and young people where there was none before. I have seen them work towards eco status and social action projects. I have seen them grow in confidence in sharing their faith in Christ with others.

The greatest effect on an MPB, however, has been where the team has continued to work on beyond the end of the larger gatherings. They have continued to work around this virtuous circle: explore, plan, act, review. They have drawn new people into the group, but kept to this overall plan together.

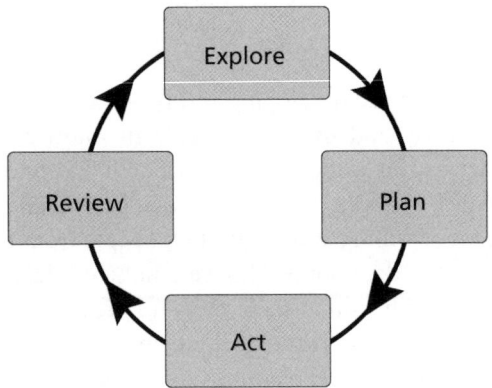

They have discovered the enormous value of a small cross-benefice action team, not replacing PCCs (Parochial Church Councils), DCCs (District Church Councils) or a Group Council, but working alongside them.

Now it is time to take the learning and the experience of those learning-and-action communities and make them more available.

The joys

The work that I, with different delivery partners, have done with learning-and-action communities was grounded in an invaluable piece of CPAS research into the realities of life for clergy in MPBs, which revealed in detail their joys and challenges (undertaken by Revd Will Donaldson). There are many joys. The potential for churches to share resources, share responsibilities and be much more than the sum of their parts by work-ing together – whether urban, suburban or rural – is enormous. There can be strength, encouragement and a release of creativity as churches support each other's initiatives and take responsibility for different parts of the ministry and mission of the whole benefice. It can work very well.

Challenges and complexity

However, I have also seen at close range the high levels of challenge and complexity facing incumbents of MPBs. I have seen clergy and leader-ship groups struggling to respond to these issues. For example:

- Should they put their energies into the older congregations who are faithful in prayer and giving, or start new things for younger people who are not yet followers of Jesus and who may not be ready to contribute to the life and financing of the Church for some time to come?
- Should they give equal attention to all the churches across the group, or focus on those where it seems there is life and the potential for growth?
- Should they spend all their energy on buildings or try to have vision for their local communities too?
- How can churches be confident and engaging in times of national and international emergency?
- What is the best way to use the digital competence that many churches have had to acquire in recent years across churches and generations of people?
- Which things being done in the churches are life-giving and should be continued, and which should be gently brought to an end?
- How can they encourage new people to become leaders in their churches and help them to flourish in those roles?
- How can churches grow when the current usual pattern for many people is to attend maybe once or twice a month rather than every week?
- How do they begin to change the culture to look at the big picture when churchgoers are often loyal to their own church and unwilling to travel to others?

- How do clergy effectively relate to many different churches and communities, manage teams, deal with multiple administrative tasks and cope with the loneliness of clergy neighbours being further away geographically?

These are vexed issues, often wearing and wearying, and there are no easy answers. However, it has been proved to me that, when a group of leaders across a benefice work together on the issues, exploring them and creating plans to tackle them, positive and creative change can happen. People's attitudes begin to change as they are inspired towards a better future.

But what about clergy roles?

The vicar looked pained. The speaker was talking about the role of clergy needing to change if churches in MPBs were to thrive. 'But,' he interrupted, unable to stay quiet any longer, 'this is not what I was called to do. It's not what I was trained to do. It's not what I want to do.'

What had been said that was so difficult?

The speaker was challenging the persistent belief of many clergy and congregations that it is possible to do ministry for four, six, ten or even more churches in the same way that it has always been done in the past with the 'one vicar, one church' model. The speaker was suggesting that the attempt by clergy to do everything, to attend every event and personally to offer pastoral care to everyone is for them a prelude to burnout, while for congregations it is a recipe for frustration. However, sometimes heroic attempts are being made to do just that because generations have expected that this is what a 'real vicar' should do.

Change is often painful, and sometimes we would rather continue with costly heroism than face challenging change. The vicar quoted above was one of many expressing the struggle and anxiety of having to rethink their roles, and of recognizing that much effort would have to go into developing other people to share in their ministry, rather than keep doing things the way they were trained to, and indeed, loved to do.

There is no doubt that MPB ministry brings many challenges. How, then, can we face the changes demanded by multi-parish ministry with creativity and vision, rather than be overwhelmed?

1 Vocation changes over time

The Spirit of God is always doing new things, and therefore God's call on us is always to grow and flex and risk doing new things, or old things in new ways, as we respond to God's leading. Lay or ordained, ready obedience to the will of God will involve change and development. If we want to stay responsive to God's call, there will always be practices that we need to lay down, good though they may have been, in order to work with God on the new things he is doing. This is harder for some than others, depending on our personality and circumstances. Take heart from the first disciples, who often discovered this in dramatic ways – think of Peter learning to include the Gentiles (Acts 10.9–23), or Philip leading the Ethiopian eunuch to faith (Acts 8.26–40).

2 There are opportunities for growth

While we may agree, albeit reluctantly, that some of the old ways are not working, there is no one sure-fire model for how to do things in multi-parish benefices that will guarantee flourishing. However, where no one individual priest can do everything any more, there are opportunities for, among many other good things:

- More shared responsibility between lay and ordained people.
- The emergence of gifts and strengths in people who maybe were unaware of them.
- Deepening of faith for many in the churches.
- A greater commitment to prayer.
- The discovery of new leaders.

3 Changing the culture of an MPB is possible

Creating culture is one of the main tasks of leaders in any organization. Whether incumbents realize it or not, the way they do and say things creates a specific culture. Where they intentionally aim at a culture that is kind, cooperative and generous, it can begin to go in that direction. Creating culture does, however, take focused attention over time.

The biggest culture change for an incumbent has to be the shift from being the main provider of ministry for one church congregation, to training and releasing others to do ministry in a multitude of churches and congregations. Many MPBs, with their clergy, realize that this is the only way to help groups of churches flourish. Others, however, are wedded to the model that has served well for many generations and find it hard to accept that the situation around them has changed so radically.

Wherever you and your churches are on that spectrum, this book and the resources that go with it will provide inspiration, practical tools and possibilities for every church to thrive.

Why is this book needed?

Thrive: Helping Your Multi-Parish Benefice to Grow aims to address what has become the norm for Church of England parishes: the grouping of parishes under one incumbent. The majority of parishes now find themselves in groups, and many now in larger groups than they were before. Nor is this just a rural reality, but true of urban and suburban churches too.

This quiet but persistent pattern of grouping parishes has meant a huge change in the Church of England, which has not been fully recognized. Currently, many dioceses are experimenting with ways to address the situation in their structures, training and deployment of leaders. Some are working with mission areas, others are reviving the practice of ordaining local leaders who stay in their patch, while others are exploring various types of lay and ordained 'focal leaders' working with oversight ministers across groups of churches. These are visionary and exciting initiatives. However, many of them will take time to bear fruit.

In the meantime, the issues around MPBs remain, many of them exacerbated by the succession of national and global crises that we have been facing in recent years. This book, and its accompanying optional resources, provide a focused structure for a group to start tackling ways to do ministry and mission more effectively across an MPB.

Facing the issues

This book is a practical response to the challenges of MPBs, a resource for those who are incumbents and others who carry significant responsibility. It explores the issues surrounding how to lead well in such settings, with examples of how others have done it.

It comes out of the journeys I have taken with courageous and committed groups of people as we have worked together in learning-and-action communities. I am endlessly grateful for all their hard work and all that I have learned from them.

The topics explored are not new and most are relevant to all churches, not just MPBs. However, the aim is to provide a structured way of looking at them from an MPB viewpoint, just as the learning-and-action communities have done. This will enable you to step back from the endless round of work and rotas, crises and dramas that are the reality of life when looking after multiple churches to discover encouraging new ways to work with others in ministry and mission across your churches.

Along the way are quotes from at-the-coalface clergy about their own experiences over the years. There are also questions at the end of each chapter to help you earth what you have read in your own context.

The Thrive collection of resources

The book can be read on its own, but it is part of a collection of resources, because experience has shown that the greatest value and potential for growth is to be found in considering these issues with other people. Only with robust discussion will realistic and visionary plans emerge for your group of churches. Only with a group will there be the energy and determination to make and put into action ideas for improving things on each topic as you study it. So do consider using one or more of the other resources outlined here in addition to reading the book.

The four Thrive: Helping Your Multi-Parish Benefice to Grow resources

The Thrive book

This book examines six different topics. The image we will work with through the book is that of a star. The centre of the star represents our praying – the most important thing we do. Each point then stands for a different area of our churches' life and mission. It is an easy way to evaluate how we are doing – at the start of the book and again at the end, once some of its recommendations have begun to be adopted. It is, however, only a starting place, a chance to look at the big picture. For ongoing change, using any or all of the other resources is highly recommended.

The Thrive Prayer Guide

The simple *Thrive Prayer Guide* is for anyone and everyone in all of the churches in an MPB who is willing to pray for the thriving of the whole group. It suggests prayer possibilities for the same six topics in the same order as in this Thrive book and in the Thrive course. It can be used in any way your churches would find helpful. For example, praying alongside the course as it runs, topic by topic; in public intercessions; in small groups; or just as it is, for individual use. It is obviously helpful if the course members and church leaders set an example by using the prayer guide in a committed way themselves.

God in his love and grace chooses his people to work alongside him in his Church and kingdom, so recruiting people to pray in a structured way for the work and outreach of your churches opens the situation up to the work of the Spirit of God who loves us dearly, invites us deeper into the Father's love and who helps us share the love of God in Christ with others. With regular praying across a benefice, we become much more open to the wind of the Spirit blowing among and through us.

The Thrive course

This fully downloadable course follows the same structure as the Thrive book, with the same six topics in the same order, and uses the star to evaluate at the beginning and the end. It is designed for a committed action team of ordained and lay leaders from across an MPB, subject to the PCCs or Group Council, who are prepared to meet regularly over the long term to put plans into action. It is designed for people who will assess and work across all of your churches, not just focus on their own church or congregation.

Each of the six topics has a PowerPoint, leaders' notes and handout for a session of group exploration and the chance to start creating an action plan around that topic. Each session – called a 'gathering' in the course – will need to be followed by regular meetings to put the action plan into practice. We suggest that it takes at least three months to work on action plans before looking at the next topic.

The course is not about heavy study, but about inspiration, activities and exercises, planning together and putting action plans into effect. The aim is to foster culture change towards a hope-filled, collaborative, outward-looking future across all of the churches in the group.

The Thrive PCC sessions

These six sessions provide interactive, sharing, discussing, planning and praying outlines for PCCs or Group Councils to help them work through some of the key issues in the book and the course. The topics concentrate on the areas that PCCs can best tackle. They are supplementary to the other resources, not completely overlapping. Of course, some people will then engage with elements of the material twice, but that means they are well placed to help discussion and planning in councils.

Time and building momentum

Whichever of these interlocking resources you choose to use, do take your time. Culture change is a long-term undertaking and so using these resources over a couple of years enables you to make changes that will last. Having said that, finding small early changes begins to build momentum and convince people that you are engaged in a worthwhile endeavour.

Local cooperation

You might consider tackling these resources – particularly the course – with another small group from a different benefice. There is often wisdom and inspiration to share between those in similar but differing circumstances. Working with others provides more momentum and accountability. It also allows for a wider team of people to do the leading of the exercises, discussions and planning in the course.

I saw this when six very varied benefices that comprised one deanery worked together in their learning-and-action community course. They tackled the task with great delight and creativity. They spurred each other on, supported each other, prayed during the difficult times and rejoiced in each other's successes.

How do the resources work together?

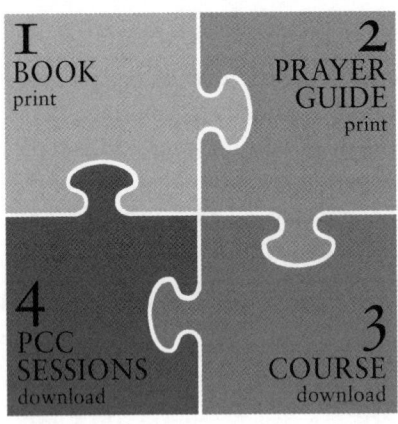

Like this Thrive jigsaw, the four elements of the collection of resources will work best when they are all in place. You could start by working through this book, answering the questions, thinking things through on your own or with one other person.

Then buy copies of the *Thrive Prayer Guide* for all the people across your churches, inviting them to start praying for your churches, perhaps starting a short online prayer meeting for the whole MPB. Include youth and older children, and younger ones, with their free downloadable worksheets.

Alongside that, or perhaps when the praying has been established for a while, start gathering your team together to do the course. You could commission the team at a benefice service if you have one and invite everyone to commit to continuing prayer.

The PCC sessions would then work best once the course is finished, to maintain momentum on reviewing some of the issues that PCCs need to keep addressing.

Which MPBs might find these resources helpful?

These resources are developed from facilitated learning communities that have run across many different dioceses, types of churches and settings. Inner-city MPBs have benefitted from them, as have suburban and deeply rural ones.

The MPBs that will find these resources most useful are those that can gather a small group of people willing to dream and plan, to act and change, in order to do their life and witness more effectively. They provide a reason and focused time to reflect and learn and plan together. With a good degree of commitment from a small group of people, they can deepen hope and open up new possibilities.

For these resources to effect real culture change, they will also work best in an MPB where the incumbent in overall charge is willing to give away both power and responsibility, while keeping people accountable. The incumbent also needs to be relaxed about the prospect of reviewing the work and life of the benefice, even when those review processes reveal difficulties.

Which MPBs might not *find these resources helpful?*

These resources are not designed for MPBs that are in a dire or dysfunctional state. Long-running feuds or the breakdown of relationships between clergy and other leaders or churches are unlikely to be sorted by using them. Other interventions, perhaps with help from senior staff in a diocese to address and resolve such issues, will be more appropriate to help an individual MPB to function in a stable manner. The leaders might then want to start looking at these resources.

Those who are looking for specific advice about the legal structure of their MPB and any changes that need to be made will not find what they need here. Again, it is worth contacting diocesan staff for help with these matters.

Those whose main current concern is the sorting of finances or buildings will also not find specific advice here. Your diocese or, for example, the Arthur Rank Centre may help: https://arthurrankcentre.org.uk.

Why should we use these resources?

These four resources will help the churches, new initiatives, groups, leaders and individuals across your churches to work together more effectively. They will encourage you to get to know one another better, to have fun together and to be more welcoming and hospitable. They will provide ideas and opportunities for helping people grow in faith and in their witness to Jesus Christ. They will begin to effect culture change and make space for the discerning and growing of new leaders, whether children, teenagers or adults. Above all, by the grace of God, these resources have the potential to engender new hope and new vision for God's work among your churches.

1

The Star

Looking at how things are now

Those who are wise shall shine like the brightness of the sky, and those who lead many to righteousness, like the stars for ever and ever. (Daniel 12.3)

'Working with this material has given people permission to think outside the box, and realize that we can do church differently.' (Quote from the coalface)

The star assessment tool

You've read the 'Start here' section. You understand how the different Thrive resources can work together. You may have found another person, or group, to discuss the book with you as you each read it. The next step is to look at how things are across your churches now.

This star assessment tool is part of both the book and the course. It captures your view of how your churches are doing in the six areas. You will be encouraged to fill in another star at the end of the book to see how things have moved on.

The six areas to consider are:

- Our Praying.
- Our Stories.
- Our Leaders.
- Our Disciples.
- Our Faith Sharing.
- Our Future.

To start things off then, please draw, on a large piece of paper, a five-pointed star, as below.

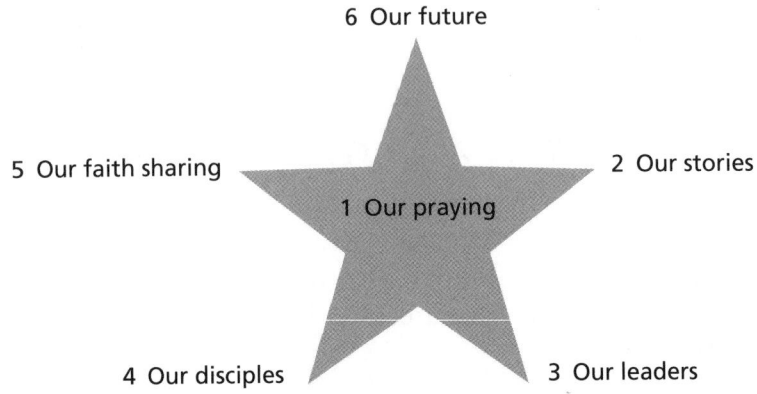

6 Our future

5 Our faith sharing

1 Our praying

2 Our stories

4 Our disciples

3 Our leaders

Take some time to think about each of these areas and assess whether they are areas of strength or weakness.

Below are some questions to get you started. Of course, just looking at the questions underlines one of the marvellous benefits of being part of a group of churches: being able to have different things going on in different churches, which the rest of the group can encourage and attend. The questions are there to start you thinking. They are certainly not there to imply that every group of churches should be doing all of these things.

1 Our praying

This is in the core of the star because it is the foundation for everything we do, and for who we aspire to be as followers of Christ. Whether our approach is formal or informal, contemplative or charismatic, loud or quiet – or a mixture across the churches – the measure of our commitment to prayer, to spending time in the presence of God individually and corporately, is a strong indicator of the health of our MPB. Praying together is one of the most encouraging things we can do as Christians, and one that opens doors for the work of God among us. How is that going across your churches?

We will look at this in Chapter 2.

2 Our stories

How are you doing across your churches on your journey of faith together? How strongly do you share a sense of direction and purpose? How well do people know the stories of your churches and how they came together? How would you describe the historic markers along the way and why they may still be having an impact on the present? How much of what goes on is about desperately trying to keep the show on the road? How well are your churches working well together and sharing resources and encouragement wherever possible?

We will look at this in Chapters 3 and 4.

3 Our leaders

How are you doing with your leaders? How much is it about trying to fill all the required positions to keep a church going? Do you have a few people, or many people, who are growing as leaders? Who has leadership responsibility in other areas of life, whom you can encourage, support and resource in their work? What training or formation opportunities, perhaps online, can you encourage those who lead in the churches and elsewhere to engage with? How are you giving children and young people opportunities to take on responsibility and lead?

We will look at this in Chapters 5 and 6.

4 Our disciples

This one is harder to measure, because often we followers of Jesus are private about our practices and disciplines. But across your group of churches, are there opportunities for people to grow in faith – Lent or Advent groups, prayer groups, Bible studies, enquirers' courses, pilgrimages or Christian meditation events, film and discussion nights and so on? Are there courses or groups for people in any specific life stages: marriage courses, Christian parenting, work-related, early retirement, older age or dementia-specific groups? Are there ways of encouraging people to develop their own disciplines of discipleship, taking responsibility for their own walk with Jesus?

We will look at this in Chapters 7 and 8.

5 Our faith sharing

How are things going in terms of sharing faith in the communities surrounding your churches? What about in people's places of work, their homes or online networks? How confident are your church people to talk about their faith with others? How keen are they to give 'an account of the hope that is in them' (1 Peter 3.15)? What are the relationships with your local schools like? If you are, wonderfully, running a food bank or toddler group, a café or a help centre, what opportunities are there to talk about what motivates you? How are you doing with any fresh expressions of church, or enquirers' events? How welcoming are your churches for those who dare to join online, or to walk through the door?

We will look at this in Chapters 9 and 10.

6 Our future

What sense of vision do you have for your churches across the benefice? Where might they be in three or five years' time? How strong is the shared sense of calling – even if that is worked out differently in each church? How hopeful are people about where you are going? Can they see beyond the next rota and the next worry about the buildings or finances? On a spectrum that ranges from actively planning for the thriving of the church for and with upcoming generations, and just struggling to keep going for one more year, how are you doing at thinking about the future across your churches? Are the better-resourced ones working with the others to help them?

We will look at this in Chapters 11 and 12.

Have fun!

This star activity is both a serious and a light-hearted exercise. As you think about these areas, or discuss them with others, mark up your big star accordingly. You might want to colour in each point of the star to an appropriate place showing which of these areas are strong and which need more work. You may want to put symbols or words in the points instead. Be as creative as you like. Whatever you do, this star then becomes a starter for you as you read the rest of the book and make use of the other resources.

When you have had the chance to work on these areas across your benefice over the course of a couple of years or more, you can revisit your star and review it. You will be able to fill in a new star showing how you have progressed in all these areas. The idea of the star may then become a reference point for future years as times and circumstances change, enabling you to keep reviewing how things are going. Sometimes ideas that seem very simple, perhaps even childlike, can open discussions in all sorts of fruitful ways.

When Jesus taught people, he used simple, everyday items and circumstances: seeds growing, lost items, sorting sheep and goats, treasure in a field and so on. Perhaps we can take this simple star and it can become a blessing in helping us shine out with the love of God into each other's lives and the lives of our communities and beyond.

In using this star in learning-and-action communities, it is so encouraging to see the difference in the beginning and ending stars for some groups. A star skimpily filled in at the beginning would compare powerfully with a much fuller and more vibrant one at the end. Sometimes a group had not noticed – while taking small, patient steps towards change over time – just how far their churches had moved on. They were filled with delight.

The opening verse in this chapter says that those who lead many to righteousness 'shine like the stars for ever and ever' (Daniel 12.3). How marvellous for the churches across our benefices to shine and lead many to the righteousness found in Jesus Christ.

2

Our Praying

Finding the foundational place

Pray in the Spirit at all times in every prayer and supplication. To that end keep alert and always persevere in supplication for all the saints. (Ephesians 6.18)

'*A top tip for a leader in an MPB? Pray! It is God's work and we need his strength.*' (Quote from the coalface)

Why start with prayer?

As the priest quoted above said: this work in a multi-parish benefice is God's work. It is all about his mission among us. It really is. We seek his will, his story. We seek 'first for the kingdom of God' as Jesus asked us to (Matthew 6.33). To do that we need to pray.

Of course, we know this. Every incumbent saying the offices, praying, wrestling with the joys and challenges of MPBs knows this. However, sometimes we lose sight of the value of praying. We get tired. Or disheartened. It is then that we remind ourselves that God invites us to be part of his story, not the other way round.

We pray because we need God's help so very much. Consider this quote:

> Our English word 'prayer' derives from the Latin *precarius*. We pray because life is precarious. We pray because life is marvellous. We pray because we find ourselves at a loss for many things, but not for the simplest words like 'please,' 'thank you,' 'wow,' and 'help.'
> (Pete Greig, *How to Pray: A Simple Guide for Normal People*, Colorado Springs, CO: NavPress, 2019)

So let's take a deep breath and start with prayer. It is the foundation of all else. Some may long for a quick fix, the latest thing that has worked elsewhere that we can import into our churches that will make everything hum with life and joy. We cast around for the one project, course or system that will deliver growth and hope. However, we know that none of this will work or be real unless it is rooted in prayer.

We remind ourselves that Jesus set the pattern for us, often spending long periods of time away from others, just with his Father in heaven, especially before big decisions (Mark 1.35–39). Often we discover that those who have significant positive impact in the world for the kingdom of God are those who quietly prioritize their conversation, and time, with God. Many are committed to the Daily Offices, or daily Eucharist. Many have explored different ways of praying at different times of their lives. Even so, it is still true that many Christian leaders, lay and ordained, across different types of church background, struggle to make time to pray a reliable, consistent priority.

We need to support and spur each other on in this. We may be doing the minimum, we may be praying a lot and loving it or we may be somewhere in between. Whatever our current experience, it is worth putting in the effort.

We remind ourselves that prayer is the heartbeat of any relationship with the God of the Bible. You cannot open many of the Bible's pages without finding his followers talking to him, listening to him. Surely Jesus spent time with his heavenly Father because he wanted to, not just because he needed to or thought he should. We know he sometimes prayed all night (Luke 6.12-13). He taught his disciples to invest in prayer (e.g. Matthew 6.5-8). He said his strength came from God. We are on solid ground if we put time with God first in our lives.

We know that none of this is easy. We may need to persevere until we find a pattern that works well for us in this season of our lives. We may need to find prayer partners, spiritual directors or soul friends. Overwhelming as it may seem, Jesus invites us to relate to him as friends (John 15.15). We know this. We know that, like the first disciples, we can walk through our days with Jesus, listening to him and expecting him to speak to us through the Scriptures, through others, through circumstances, thoughts and events. God is never limited in the ways he will speak to us as we become more used to listening out for him. We teach this to others but still, we have to admit, sometimes we are preaching to ourselves as much as to anyone else.

To underline this again, we will only see growth in our own lives and across our MPBs as we learn to be prayerful people. We are invited, always, to live more and more in awareness of the Spirit of God at work in us and through us. On the miserable days and on the happy days. When we are productive and when we are resting. When we are filled with joy and when we are burdened by life.

One curate was feeling guilty that the only time he had to pray was the half an hour each evening of walking up and down with the baby on his shoulder, helping the child go to sleep. He came to realize that this was a good starting point – to make the most of that time, rather than beating himself up that it was the only time.

Is it time to revisit the books, articles, talks, courses, apps and websites that may help us to pray? Time to remind ourselves that this journey will be lifelong; that there is always more to discover, try, explore and learn? What an extraordinary privilege that we are invited to live our lives in conversation with God. If your prayer life has become stale, then do whatever you need to do to refresh it.

The lost art of intercession?

For our purposes in helping our benefices to thrive and grow, in the rest of this chapter we concentrate on intercession. We will consider other kinds of prayer in Chapter 8.

Here we think of praying for our churches. There are obvious things we can pray for:

- Each church in our MPB, for its life and witness.
- The precious people in our MPB, for their own walk with God and their growth in faith.
- The work that these people do and the places they go.
- That God, in Christ, 'spreads in every place the fragrance that comes from knowing him' in every network our people are part of, both physical and virtual, and whoever they are with (2 Corinthians 2.14).
- The communities around each of our churches, whether urban, suburban or rural, for their well-being and flourishing.

- The work that the churches do to bless their communities, for specific areas of need.

This intercession is a responsibility that all lay and ordained church leaders carry. It does not have to be complicated, but ideally it will be regular and committed. It may be that we have lost confidence or have allowed disappointment to wear us down. When our prayers are answered with a 'no' or a 'not yet', it is easy for the discouragement to drain our hearts of hope. If so, then let us seek out some encouraging stories from other situations to ignite our own hope and faith again, and prioritize building up our trust in God's good purposes.

Committed, uncomplicated daily prayer

Not only do we have a responsibility to pray, but also to help those in our churches to discover how best *they* do committed and uncomplicated daily prayer. For some that will be in quietness and stillness. For others that will be while being active – doing housework, being outside, gardening, walking. Whatever will work best for people at this time in their lives is what we can help them to discover.

Using the Thrive Prayer Guide

Encouraging people to use the *Thrive Prayer Guide* will help people to be focused in their praying for your churches. Some will use it just for a short while, others may commit to it for the long term. Your intercessors may well really enjoy using it. Do encourage people to be committed and creative in the ways that they pray, to keep their praying fresh and varied.

Telling the stories

Finally, there is nothing like hearing stories of answered prayer to encourage people to pray and not give up. So as leaders, find ways to help people talk about moments when prayers for the churches, people and communities have led to real change. Obviously, care for confidentiality and safeguarding needs to be at the forefront here. It is about encouraging people to tell their own stories rather than hijacking their stories for our own use, or putting undue pressure on people. As the stories are told, others are inspired to bring their concerns to God.

For example, one church started praying specifically and persistently, publicly and privately, for more families, children and young people to join them, and, as the weeks passed, family by family, they started to come.

Innovative ideas from others

When we have talked about praying for our churches in learning communities for MPBs, a number of innovative ideas have emerged. These are some:

1 Inviting people to join online morning or evening prayer every day or for specific days each week, and praying always for the work of the churches in the intercessions.
2 Writing a prayer for their benefice, to be used in the intercessions at every service across their group. After a while, changing the prayer to keep things fresh.
3 Setting up prayer groups for specific topics, for a specific length of time – perhaps during Lent or Advent, or just for the summer term.
4 Creating a safe place for people to light a candle to pray in the churches, and pens and sticky notes to write prayers.
5 Setting aside a week for 24/7 prayer – with people signing up to pray for an hour to cover every hour of the day and night.
6 Creating a time-limited prayer commitment for people to sign up to. Six months of daily praying, or in Advent leading up to the Christmas services that often have many visitors, with a priority on praying for the churches and their witness.
7 Prayer walking round parts or all of the benefice – an especially enjoyable family activity during the summer.
8 Making space in services for silent prayer and the contemplation of our call to join in God's mission.
9 Inviting people across the benefice, or in already established house groups, to do a course together learning about prayer.

10 Having an online or onsite weekly prayer meeting and keeping it
    creative and well paced, with different ways of doing intercessions,
    to keep people interested and committed.

Spotting the intercessors

As you encourage people to pray for the churches, you may well spot
people across your churches who seem to have a particular gift for intercession. They are people who, somehow or other, have found that they
love to pray, that they have an instinct to spend significant time praying
for people, churches and situations. You get the impression that when
they say, 'I'll pray for you', they follow through on their promise very
seriously.

They may well be unnoticed in what they do – but when you come
across them, do encourage them. They may not want any kind of
limelight, but do thank them for their praying. Do ask them to pray
specifically for the work and witness of the churches, both inherited
and fresh expressions, across your MPB, and to make use of the *Thrive
Prayer Guide*.

These intercessors may also be people who receive particular wisdom
from God as they pray. Listen to them and take note, weighing carefully
what they say. And again, encourage them, for theirs is sometimes a
costly and hidden calling.

Fasting

In talking about intercession, it is also worth looking at fasting. After
all, Scripture often references prayer in association with fasting. There
are excellent books around that treat this in detail, but as incumbents
or lay leaders of churches, we need to think and talk about fasting, for
ourselves and with our congregations.

This is a challenge in a culture that idolizes instant gratification. I
wonder when we last encouraged people to abstain from something –
whether it be food, always-on technology, an all-consuming hobby or
some other thing – in order to devote time to God in prayer? In a society
that prizes self-actualization and self-fulfilment, this is not a popular
course of action, but it is one we need to re-learn. Who knows what joys

we miss for not seeking the presence of God as our first priority? Fasting – sensibly and carefully – is a symbol of our longing for more of God at work in our lives and churches. Why not explore with your churches the meaning of fasting – perhaps during Lent – and encourage people to fast and pray for all the churches in your group?

When we pray ...

Whatever you choose, when people pray for their churches regularly, it begins to have an impact. One teenager, who had come to faith from an unchurched background, reflected on his Christian journey with his local church and said: 'I am so glad I get to spend the rest of my life with Jesus because of this church.'

Questions to consider

We can only start from where we are. Take a moment to make an honest inventory of your prayer life, and the ways you are encouraging others to pray.

1　Are you praying, steadily and persistently, creatively and committedly, for the work and witness of your churches? Are you praying for people to discover the love of God in Jesus? Are you praying for the communities in which your churches are set – whether they are villages, towns or cities? Are you giving yourself time to learn more about intercession?

2　When did you last speak to a spiritual director or close friend about your praying, to help you be more attentive to the presence and work of God in your life?

3　What resources are there in your diocese for spiritual accompaniment? How would you find out more?

4　When did you last give people an opportunity, perhaps with just a couple of others so it is not too intimidating, to share stories about their own praying and the ways God has answered their prayers?

5 How could you encourage others on their prayer journeys?

6 What might you do across your MPB to deepen the work of intercession for your churches and communities?

If clergy and lay leaders of churches and fresh expressions are prepared to take prayer seriously, then it is easier to encourage others to do so. Those who discover the delight of spending time in God's presence can inspire others as well. Those who are persistent in prayer even in the dry times can help others through their difficulties.

It remains a mystery that God invites us into his presence through prayer, but what a privilege it is. As one bishop said to me years ago: 'I don't care how you pray, but you *must* pray.'

Story time

An MPB group of leaders invited people from all their churches to set an alarm at an agreed time of day for people to stop for a couple of minutes and pray for the MPB. One church leader told of sitting in a meeting with some outside agencies when her prayer alarm went off. Instead of hushing the alarm and just continuing with the meeting, she put down her cuppa, explained to those present what the alarm was about, asked if they minded joining her in a prayer, and, with their consent, prayed briefly for the churches in the MPB she led. Not all of those present were Christians – although they were gathered on church business – but all saw the commitment to the well-being of those churches in the actions of that leader. The others who had also committed to pray were much encouraged by her example.

3

Our Stories, Part 1

Mapping our stories, past, present and future

'Know therefore that the LORD your God is God, the faithful God who keeps covenant and steadfast love with those who love him and keep his commandments, to a thousand generations.' (Deuteronomy 7.9 ESV)

'With each village being like a distinct individual, through its history and composition, multi-church ministry demands a reflectiveness and sensitivity to difference and possibility.' (Quote from the coalface)

Our story

In this chapter we explore the stories of our churches. As we plan for the future, it helps enormously to look back and trace our journey to the present, while taking into account the influences along the way. We will look at the stories of our churches at three levels. First, we will think about the stories of our wider culture in recent decades. This will set the scene.

Second, we will think about changes in the Church of England. What has been happening in recent decades that has changed the landscape? What are some of the trends, debates and realities that have gone into shaping our churches and MPBs today?

Third, and most importantly, we will explore the stories of our own MPB. How and when did our churches come together? Is it a simple story or one full of twists and turns? As we untangle the story and look at its highs and lows, we will understand the current situation more clearly. In addition, we will begin to see more clearly how we might grow in our work together across the benefice as disciples of Jesus Christ, showing and sharing the love of God with each other and our communities.

1 The stories of our culture

Many people have written about the sweeping changes we have seen across our culture over the past decades. However, there is great value in exploring this with people within MPBs. It is easy for churches to fall into one of two difficult traps in response to culture change. The first is to minimize it and then feel that, if their group of churches is struggling, it is all their fault. Nothing can ever change. The second is to pay too much attention to the issues in our wider society, believe that our changing culture is to blame for every ill in our churches and then also conclude that nothing can ever improve.

Of course, both of these responses are partly true. We do have to bear some responsibility for not finding effective ways of passing on our faith to younger generations. We do need to repent, as church leaders, of not helping people to become disciples of Jesus. It is also true that cultural changes have had huge impact on churches, marginalizing them so that they have become just one option in an increasingly wide range of 'spiritual' offerings for those seeking purpose and meaning in life. However, the bigger picture is always that our God has good purposes for us and our churches, whichever of these attitudes we have embraced or are in danger of embracing.

We can have courage and confidence in those good purposes as we develop vision across our churches. Think of the extraordinary declaration Jesus made in Matthew 16.18: 'And I tell you, you are Peter, and on this rock I will build my church, and the gates of Hades will not prevail against it.'

Stand your ground

The stories of our culture are ones of constant change. Our lives are played out against a backdrop of huge national, international and even global events. Whether world politics, pandemic, war or climate change and natural disasters, recent years have seen us recognizing our own fragility and mortality anew. There has been grief, fear and sorrow, perhaps on a scale most of us have not known before.

Exploring these changes is helpful for everyone in our churches. You could do it as an exercise together. Ask people, in small groups, to list all the big changes – good and bad – they have seen during their lifetime, then share all your ideas together. You could do this as part of an MPB vision day. However, be warned: once groups get started on it, they might be hard to stop – especially the oldest people who have, obviously, experienced the most changes. Encourage people to resist the temptation to get stuck on just the difficult changes, for there are many that are astonishingly good (note that this exercise is included in the downloadable Thrive course).

If you do such an exercise, these are some of the things that might emerge.

1 Changes in technology

This is often the first one we think of, because it is the most far-reaching. From the arrival of the television to the invention of the smartphone – plus the knowledge of all the things in the pipeline – we are in a very different world from the one many people knew growing up. Much of the technological change is exciting, creative and wildly helpful. Where would we have been during the pandemic without the ability to have safe online meetings when many of us were working from home? What a blessing to be able to keep in touch with family and friends far and wide and stay close to them through sharing our lives online.

However, we also know the downsides of technology: people becoming addicted to the 'always-on' culture; parents ignoring children to check their phones; damagingly addictive viewing of unhelpfully available content on the internet; the dangers and struggles that come from social media – to mention just a few. As always with human inventions, great steps forward are accompanied by more sinister possibilities.

2 Changes in religion

This one is easy to see – and a cause of great grief for many. The days when most people in the UK had at least a basic understanding of Christian faith are long gone. Devout parents have watched their children and grandchildren move further and further away from the faith they knew as children. The perceived war between science and God has convinced many that the two are completely incompatible, with the Christian genesis of science conveniently forgotten. The Church is often viewed as out of touch and out of date and rarely regarded as somewhere to go to discover the meaning of life. People often describe themselves as 'spiritual but not religious'.

The other big religious change, as well as a move towards secularism, is the prevalence of other religions. In an increasingly multicultural society, we are all more likely to know people of other faiths and no faith. The latter may have picked up practices from a kaleidoscope of sources to help them through life: some non-Christian meditation; some hope of reincarnation; some discipline of gratitude, to name but a few. These changes often cause Christians to be wary of talking about their faith, lest they find themselves in waters that are too deep to swim in, or they be accused of prejudice.

In these practices, both the ones with roots in other religions and those that are recommended as healthy psychological disciplines, it seems that, useful as some of them may be, they are ultimately about looking to be saved and healed without a saviour. For example, it is a wonderful thing to learn disciplines of daily gratitude – and many recommend it. However, it only finds its true riches and depth when we know the One to be grateful to, as we find in Philippians 4.6-7:

> Do not be anxious about anything, but in every situation, by prayer and petition, with thanksgiving, present your requests to God. And the peace of God, which transcends all understanding, will guard your hearts and your minds in Christ Jesus. (NIV)

Again, mindfulness is a helpful discipline for many – but centuries of Christian meditation witness to a depth of encounter and love that is much more significant than mindfulness. And, ultimately, of course, we Christians will testify to the regular experience of God's love and forgiveness that we know as followers of Jesus – forgiveness opened up for us in the story of Jesus and his death and resurrection.

3 Suspicion of institutions

Alongside changes in religious practice is a more widespread suspicion of institutions of any kind, and especially of their leaders. Trust in politics and politicians has waned through scandals and lying behaviour. It is not just the Church that has been held up for scrutiny, but all leadership, whether civic, educational, local or business. People in public service roles are quickly held to account. The power of social media to undermine and destroy the reputations of people and organizations has left few areas of national life untouched.

This leaves people longing for authenticity, for leaders in every sphere whom they can trust to act with integrity. The challenge to all church denominations is serious, but so it is for every other institution.

4 Social and family changes

At the same time as all the changes in technology, the rise of secularism and other faiths, there are huge social changes going on around us: changing approaches to the understandings of family life, human sexuality and gender identity; the recognition of the appalling injustices of racial prejudice. These have all brought sweeping changes in attitudes that have had powerful effects on our culture and ways of life. Some of these are liberating, good and fair. They are just as important for Christians as everyone else. Some lead us to question and wonder and disagree, among ourselves as well as with others.

5 Educational changes

It is also worth noting all the changes in education across the decades. Some in our churches may remember schooling as an individual endeavour, seated at single desks, learning what the teacher taught. So much has changed since then. Schools now are more likely to seat children around tables with others, to learn and tackle projects together, exploring topics rather than just being told what to do. Schools give children more and more opportunities to lead, to take responsibility, to speak in public, to be part of school councils.

It is crucial that we in the churches understand these changes. Children and young people today are rightly not content just to be told what to think and do. At school, they are encouraged to question, to explore, to discover and to reach their own conclusions. At church, they will expect to do the same. More of this anon, but for the moment we recognize that this is a significant change in how people are being formed as they go through the educational system.

6 Political and international changes

There are so many more changes we could mention – the ups and downs of the economy, Brexit and its consequences, the effects of political upheaval, climate change, the 24-hour news cycle, and on and on. The international scene changes almost day by day. The upheavals come thick and fast and, because we can hear news almost the moment it happens, people of all generations can easily become overwhelmed and afraid.

What effects do these changes have?

These are significant changes within the stories of our culture. Each is worthy of serious examination, but that is not the purpose here. Simply, it is to acknowledge the complexities of church life in a world that is changing so rapidly.

Living in such a fast-changing world can leave Christians feeling beleaguered and defensive. Many have summed up the changes by saying that the age of 'Christendom' has passed, and they fear what is here and what is to come instead.

And yet, and yet, that is not the whole picture. Sometimes, from within our church communities, especially perhaps within those that are struggling to stay afloat, we see things more dismally than is actually the case. There is consistent research showing that there are people who would love to try coming to church, or exploring Christian faith, if someone would only invite them to do so (see the report from the Talking Jesus website, https://talkingjesus.org/2022-research). Again, the attitudes towards Christians in the workplace or in life generally are much more positive than we suspect. All is far from lost. And because there are many who are yet to hear the story of the Christian faith, there is the potential for huge impact as it comes to them brand new. Challenges to the story of truth have always existed and Jesus reminds us that 'In this world you will have trouble. But take heart! I have overcome the world' (John 16.33 NIV).

However, the point is that the stories of the culture and world around us have been defined by rapid change during our lifetimes – whatever age we are – and the speed of change does not look like slowing any time soon. This is the context of our life and witness as groups of churches. How can we help our churches to thrive in working together, in sharing faith with each other, and with those who want to know more, in ways that are wholesome and effective in a complex world?

2 The stories of the Church of England

Our denomination is continually changing and developing. Although many perhaps love to think that, in a rapidly changing world, the Church of England is unchanging and safe, a quick look at recent decades shows that that is far from the case. As it has to do in every age, the Church is trying to react well to circumstances, remain faithful to its core message and shape itself well for the future. This is never a simple process and there are many twists and turns along the way as there always will be. There are six particular things that are of interest to us here.

1 Speaking of faith

The first change is the gradual, wider acceptance of the need for churches to become communities that show and share their faith – not just on Sundays, but every day of the week. No longer can we assume that people will come to us to find out about God. No longer can we assume that people know what it means to be a disciple of Jesus Christ nor even know the underlying stories of the Christian faith. We need to become those who can give a reason for the hope that is within us (1 Peter 3.15). We are in circumstances more like those of the earliest

Christians – working out our faith in a culture that is largely ignorant about Christianity, and sometimes antagonistic.

2 Varieties of services

The second change is to the pattern of services. The Parish Communion Movement, which started and flourished in the twentieth century, encouraged churches to have a service of Holy Communion as their main service every week. Before that, the standard diet in Church of England churches was Morning and Evening Prayer, with Holy Communion perhaps as an early service or as an occasional optional addition to a mid-morning service. Anglicans across many traditions have therefore come to treasure taking communion weekly.

However, with the reduction in numbers of clergy, and the increase in MPBs, the success of this movement has brought some unintended consequences. In many MPBs there are not enough priests – even with the help of retired ones – for every church to have Holy Communion as its main service every week. 'Communion by extension', where a lay reader distributes bread and wine consecrated at an earlier time by a priest, is probably happening more often than the guidelines allow.

This raises questions around ordination that dioceses are responding to in different ways. Some are renewing schemes to provide Ordained Local Ministers. Some are ordaining lay readers. Many are recognizing the need to have a wider variety of services – especially lay-led Services of the Word. Although there are churches that have been doing this for years, for others this is a new venture, and some dioceses have training schemes to help lay leaders flourish in delivering such services.

3 Mixed ecology

The third big change is the growing understanding of the need for a 'mixed ecology' of Church, with different types of services and churches. There is increasing recognition that one size does not fit all and that we need a variety of styles of churches – inherited, fresh expressions of church, church plants, resource churches – in order to help people find a way of exploring and discovering faith in Jesus in a way that works for them. This has meant large amounts of investment of money, time, prayer and effort to try new things. There has been impressive energy for creative initiatives, which have resulted in many people becoming parts of new worshipping communities who would not have considered coming to inherited churches. The ones that most people have heard of are Messy church and café church, but there are many others. At the same time, the more traditional-style churches are exploring ways of reaching out more and being a blessing to their communities, through thoughtful hospitality, increasing the variety of services they offer, doing more social action and inviting people to come.

4 More multi-parish benefices

The fourth big change that particularly affects our considerations here is, of course, that MPBs have become widespread. Over recent decades, what was initially expedient in individual cases – the grouping of parishes under one leader – has become the norm. A majority of parishes now find themselves in groups, whether urban, suburban or rural.

Much of this is driven by finance, with the decreasing numbers of full-time clergy. These are serious and challenging realities that are unlikely to ease in the short term. So our question then becomes: 'How can we live faithfully and fruitfully as disciples of Jesus across our groupings of parishes during times of pressure and uncertainty?' How can we work well together across our group of churches to grow in our faith, to demonstrate the love of God in our communities and to help people discover the love of God for themselves?

When we add in the challenging facts that many of our Sunday congregations have few younger people and our older saints are weary, the situation is far from easy. Having said that, in the CPAS learning communities for MPBs over recent years, it is noticeable that it is often these older saints who are both the most prayerful people and the most radical in what they want to risk in order to help their churches grow and flourish. This is not to return to some 'golden age' of the past, but to see what God is doing next and join in with it.

5 *More and more leaders*

The fifth change is that we are discovering that we need many more church leaders. This is not just because numbers of full-time clergy have been decreasing, but also because, as churches are put together in groups, and new churches and fresh expressions of church are planted, they need leaders. Report after report to the General Synod of the Church of England over recent decades calls passionately for more lay leaders. We will explore this more in the chapters about leaders, but it is a huge culture change in the Church, which is happening slowly and often against some resistance.

6 *Abuse and safeguarding*

Another far-reaching change has been the revelations of abuse by Christians and Christian leaders. The courageous revelations of survivors are deeply distressing and a necessary exposé of the misuses of power. Naturally, and understandably, confidence in the Church has been significantly undermined.

In the wake of these sinful attitudes and behaviours coming to light, the Church – as every other institution – is putting its safeguarding house in order. This essential change is no small undertaking. In ten years' time, safeguarding checks will be normal, but it is currently a challenging upheaval to bring every church up to date with its safeguarding practice. In an MPB, those tasks are multiplied, often with real reluctance and misunderstanding of the need to comply. For clergy and lay leaders, there is the need to be constantly vigilant, plus anxiety about mishandling any disclosures that come their way.

3 The local stories of our MPB

Of all the stories we are considering, that of our own MPB is perhaps the most important. Yes, we know that culture has changed around us – and the longer we have lived, the more changes we have seen. Yes, we know that the Church of England is also continually changing, in small, often unnoticed ways, as well as in big, sweeping changes. However, what we may not actually know is the story of how our churches came together.

It is worth learning that story because it affects the present state of our MPB in a variety of ways. In most cases, the story is not simple or straightforward. Sometimes individual churches have been moved from one grouping to another over time. Sometimes smaller groupings have been brought together in a larger one, with all sorts of attendant stresses and strains. Sometimes, there are even echoes of historic family feuds across churches that destabilize the present. One group I met with very recently were still being affected by the fact that churches in their group had been on different sides during the Civil War in the seventeenth century. Strange but true.

Again, it may be that ancient boundaries – county and occasionally even country boundaries – have been summarily crossed in the creation of an MPB that causes difficulties in the present. Even geographical features, such as a hill or river or major road, can be part of the story and affect the way the churches in a group relate to each other. Yet other churches will look back with longing to a perceived golden age when their church was full and growing. All of these stories, the good and the sad, are worth sharing and hearing so that your churches – whether they have just come together or have been working together for a long time – can know and understand and pray for each other in good and healthy ways.

The exploration of the story of your MPB does not have to be a grim and serious enterprise. Conversations with people across the churches will begin to create a picture not just of the challenges but also of the joys along the way. As you explore, you may well find stories of churches delighting to get to know each other in a group, feeling much more supported by being together rather than feeling like a small outpost of the Church of England. You may well find histories of times when churches putting on initiatives together was much more fun and fruitful than trying to go it alone, or when a larger church supported a smaller one in specific ways.

Our current stories – joys and challenges

Researching and understanding the past stories of a group of churches makes it easier to see more clearly their place in the big stories of the changes in the wider culture and in our denomination. You can perhaps begin to clarify historical, geographical and socio-economic reasons for how things are now.

The next task, then, is to explore your current stories. What are the joys and challenges across your churches that you would identify? It's a question you could raise with others: PCCs, housegroups, coffee-morning attendees, youth clubs, Messy-church people, church wardens and people outside the churches. Remember to ask people of all ages.

As you take note of their answers, the stories of your churches become richer and fuller. Areas of need come more clearly into focus. Stories of joy, hope and encounter with God emerge.

Of buildings, money and dioceses

By way of a short detour, we must acknowledge that many of the answers that come our way will be about the challenges of maintaining historic buildings, about how to keep finances coming in and how to relate to a diocese facing its own financial and staffing struggles. These are huge issues and vary so much from place to place that they are not our focus in this book. Our priority is to look at how churches can work well together across a benefice and strengthen their faith and witness. So as you ask the questions about how the churches in your MPB are now, do give due weight to the answers about buildings and finance, but help people to consider matters beyond those issues. Encourage them to consider deeper questions about the morale of the churches, about how well they are working together and the joys of their stories as individual churches and as part of the benefice.

Telling the stories of faith

We will be thinking about ways of sharing our faith in later chapters, but for now, as you unearth stories about churches and individuals, perhaps this is the time to start sharing the good reports of what God is doing across your churches and communities. Are there people willing to write the story of what their church means to them, or record a short video for your website? Perhaps they would speak up in a special service about what God has recently done in their lives, or about answers to prayer they have seen.

As we begin to tell current stories of what God is doing across our churches and in the lives of individuals, we help people make the connections between what they read of the God active in the Bible and the real ordinary lives of Christians today, encountering God in their everyday world. As faith grows, we all grow in confidence in telling our stories and more people become interested as the stories are told more widely. The atmosphere can change and people on the fringes of our churches can become more interested. The gossip about our churches begins to spread in the communities, and we all become more alert to the opportunities to talk about faith in our normal lives.

The story to come

Having explored the historical stories of our culture, our denomination and our local churches and communities in recent decades, you may also have found out what people of all ages think about your churches now. The biggest challenge of all, however, is to start working on the story that is to come. What is God calling you all to next? How might your churches work together on that? Just to remind you: this book and the accompanying Thrive collection of resources, should you choose to use them, all aim to take you further along that path.

Whatever you do, please set aside time to think about and plan for the story you hope God will write in and through your churches in the years to come. MPB life can be so relentless and demanding that, without deliberately putting time aside to explore the story so far, the story now and the story to come, church life becomes all about keeping the plates spinning rather than engaging with the adventure God calls us to.

Questions to consider

Exploring these stories – our culture, the Church of England and our own benefices and communities – can be an energizing and fascinating journey of discovery. These questions are offered to help you get going:

1 What is your own understanding of the stories across these three areas? Perhaps write down what you think before you start asking others, and then compare this with some research. That will make very clear what you have learned.

2 What themes have emerged about the history of your benefice as you have asked around? Is there anything you did not know already? Is there anything surprising? Is there anything you need to address urgently?

3 What has delighted you as you have talked with people? Where do you see God at work? Are you encouraging people to tell their current stories of what it means to them to follow Jesus?

4 As you go through the rest of this book, how will you keep questioning where the story God is writing in your churches is going next?

5 Are you still praying for your churches regularly and asking others to do so too?

Story time

As you listen for the stories of joys and challenges across your benefice, make sure to ask the youngest and the oldest. For example, I came across one rural church where two five-year-old girls were pestering endlessly for a club for their age group because they saw church-based clubs across a benefice for older children and teenagers. They got it eventually. It took too long, but at least their enthusiasm was recognized and catered for.

When a new leader came to a smaller, suburban benefice, they started researching with others the stories of the churches. What was revealed was some long-held and rather bitter resentment of one church – which had been built for the workers – against another church – built for the owners and managers of local businesses. Gradually, through dialogue, prayer and a service of reconciliation, generational grievances were apologized for, forgiven and laid to rest, opening up a new and happier future for all the churches involved.

4

Our Stories, Part 2

Relating well across the group

Love one another with mutual affection; outdo one another in show-ing honour. (Romans 12.10)

'Our churches relate to one another like a dysfunctional family. We'd like to change that to be more like a team.' (Quote from the coalface)

Stories and relationships

The stories of churches in MPBs over the years – both within individual churches and across the churches – are always made up of relationships: relationships between individuals and between different congregations. In this chapter, having looked at the big stories of the wider culture, the Church of England and of the benefice, the focus is local stories. It starts with asking some big questions, then looks at different metaphors and models for relating together and ends with suggestions for building trust between people and churches.

Why do these churches exist?

The starting point is that little question that children ask so readily, and that we as adults forget to ask: 'Why?' It is time to ask: 'Why do the churches in this benefice exist?' The question here is not about the buildings, which may have been constructed for all sorts of worthy and less worthy reasons, with a short or long history. You may have discovered more about that as you looked at the stories of your churches and benefice. The focus now is on why all these groups of followers of Jesus exist – whether they meet in a church building or a school or somewhere else.

The challenge of this exercise is to approach it from different viewpoints. You could do this exercise yourself and then ask others the same questions to find out how their answers compare with yours. To do this well, you need to be very honest in your answers.

The viewpoints to consider are:

1   What might God think about why these churches exist?
2   What do the clergy and lay leaders think about why these churches exist?
3   What do the congregations of these churches think about why they exist?
4   What do the people in the local community think about why the churches exist?
5   What would a complete stranger coming into one of your services or gatherings think about why these churches exist?

Having attempted to answer these questions, look at the answers and see how much numbers 2–5 align with what you believe to be the answers to number 1. What might you do to bring those answers more into alignment? How can the story that people see being lived by your individual churches, and the benefice as a whole, reflect God's purposes more fully?

Getting to know each other

Having thought about why the churches exist, the next question to consider is how the people in the churches relate to one another. Of course, the complexity of the responsibilities for clergy and lay leaders in MPBs is significant. Alongside all the big issues we looked at in the last chapter is the endless march of demands, services, rotas, pastoral crises, tricky relationships, competing congregations, growing initiatives, difficult conversations and all the other things that make up the day-by-day life of MPBs.

With all of that going on, we may find the 'softer' issues – like people getting to know each other, relating well to one another across the group of churches and doing more things together – are easily relegated to the bottom of the list. Surely the main need is for some hard-headed realism about the situations we face, great management and some bold decision-making?

Yes, of course we need to be realistic, and of course we need to manage the issues we face well, and make difficult decisions. However, we also need to keep our eye on the long-term goals. Our priorities must be to help people grow as disciples and to explore new outreach initiatives with the strength of numbers that comes from working together.

For example, one group of churches, by joining together for their evening Holy Week services, had enough people present to make it worth inviting some excellent outside speakers. No one church in the group could have done that alone, but together they had an encouraging and profound time, returning to their own church buildings for the Good Friday and Easter services.

You may be in a well-established MPB, or one that has just had more churches added to it. You may be in one that has just come together. Whichever is true, it is worth pondering how you relate to one another and how those relationships could deepen. This is not so that you spend all your time across the MPB looking inwards. It is rather to identify how best to love and bless one another, encouraging one another in worship, witness and service.

How do the churches in your group relate to each other? Metaphors and models

How do your churches relate across the group at the moment? Is it the way you would like it to be? As always, it is good to know where you are starting from and how you would like that to change.

The following are two ways of looking at the relationships between the people in your churches.

1 Metaphors for our relationships

Think about these four different metaphors in relation to your group of churches. As you read through, ask yourself which one most clearly resonates with what you experience of your churches. It's unlikely that any one will be quite right, maybe a mixture of two or more. It's also possible that you will think of a completely different metaphor that works better for your group of churches, but these can be used as a jumping off point.

1 A jazz band

In a jazz band, each musician makes their own contribution. As a band, they have an agreed shape to the music and sometimes they play together and sometimes each musician has a chance to be the soloist. They have to listen carefully to each other and support each person's contribution. There is lots of improvisation along the way based around the agreed facts of the music: who the leader is; any changes of key or time signature; the basic chord progression; the original melody; and who plays when.

Are your churches a bit like this?

2 Children playing happily in a circle

The children here are a mixed group playing happily together, not minding that one child has temporarily broken the ring in her excitement. They are enjoying being together and including one another. They seem to agree what they are doing without one child obviously being in charge, although there is probably someone. They seem to be co-operating on an equal basis.

Are your churches a bit like this?

3 Circus performers

Here everyone has their own well-developed skills and gifts. They are encouraged to develop to their full potential by the ringmaster. Together, their highly specialized, different types of work make something creative, attractive and involving, but it is all quite individualistic and may be very competitive. The ringmaster is the final arbiter. Behind the scenes are many people enabling the spectacle with their administrative, financial, marketing and organizational skills. Circuses are also traditionally very committed communities, travelling together.

Are your churches a bit like this?

4 Independent allotment gardeners

These allotment gardeners want to get on with working their own patch. They do not want to waste time chatting or cooperating. In fact, they are rather hostile to one another. They are only interested in their own plot. They pay their rent to the council and get on with the job. Here, there is no sharing of wisdom and information, no helping out or lending of tools, no giving out of surplus produce. Occasionally they acknowledge each other, but that's as good as it gets.

Are your churches a bit like this?

2 Models of relationships

Another more analytical way of looking at the way our churches work together is through models. These models are more specific. They describe ways of talking about vision for a benefice and of helping people understand and commit to that vision.

Again, as we go through these, think about how they might relate to your churches and the way they relate formally and informally to each other.

No one model fits every group situation – life is just not that tidy. There may be resonance in one or more of them, but they are at least a useful starting place for discussion.

1 A minster model

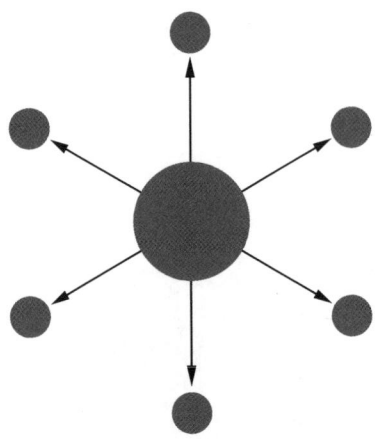

This is probably the most well-known model. It suits a group where one church is dominant. Often this is a larger church than the others and it has an agreed role of facilitating and resourcing the smaller units. It is the focal point. Sometimes this model is used in an ecumenical way, like a large Vineyard church resourcing a number of small Anglican ones. The smaller units will relate to each other in various ways, so other lines could be drawn between all if necessary.

At best, the minster model works well when there is a high degree of trust between churches that enables them all – small and large – to grow.

At worst, the reliance on the minster creates a dependency culture. It also assumes that the dominant church has a missional focus and that therefore all the arrows point outwards. However, sometimes a larger church in an MPB actually draws all the resources into itself, rather than giving out to smaller churches.

Do you recognize your churches in this model?

2 A federal or cluster model

A federal model suits a group where each church enjoys similar status but where some might have special ministries that contribute to the whole. This may describe a new benefice of similar-sized churches, each with its own strong identity. They are, however, beginning to learn to work together, support each other and grow as disciples and leaders together.

A federal or cluster model needs a high degree of developed leadership to work well, and training and contributing to the whole becomes of paramount importance.

At best, this model retains autonomy for individual units but within a corporate vision.

At worst, federal systems use the time and energy of clergy and lay leaders badly. Strategic thinking is sometimes squashed by the pressure to maintain the status quo, even if it is declining. Also, the identity of individual churches is very strongly rooted in each place rather than across the bigger picture. A successful movement towards thinking to a corporate and federal mindset is a hard one for many parishes to make.

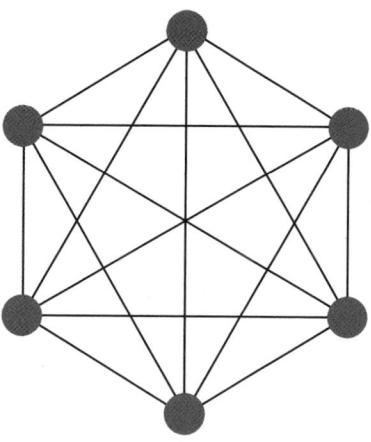

Do you recognize your churches in this model?

3 A franchise model

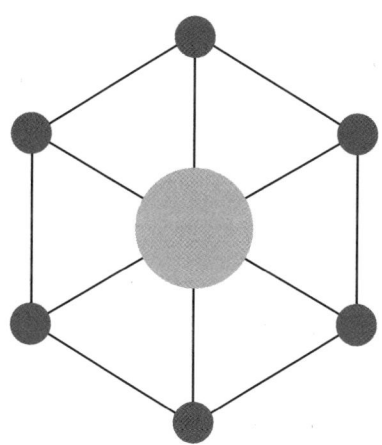

This model works where a group of churches will have some form of Group Council that sets policy and agrees parameters for values and vision within the group. Once this is agreed, each church is then free to work in its own locality by pursuing the central aims in the most locally appropriate way. No one church feeds the group. Rather, the churches cooperate to formulate a core vision and then each church works out the implications of this core vision in its own context.

Legally, it's the council that holds the vision and many people will have a greater sense of this wider vision and of churches working together.

At best, the balance between over-arching vision and values and the work of individual churches is creatively maintained, with all heading in the same overall direction.

At worst, this model can become competitive, or overwhelmed by the weight of the central council, to the detriment of the life and witness of individual churches and fresh expressions of church.

Do you recognize your churches in this model?

4 A hybrid model

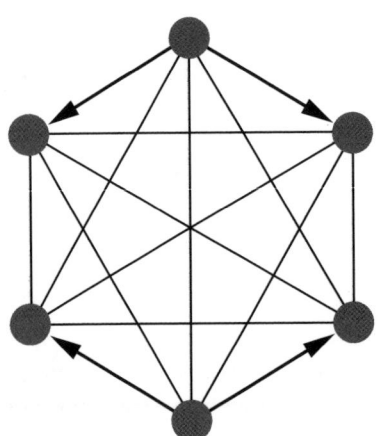

A hybrid model is a mixture of the minster and federal models. It suits a group where there may be more than one dominant church, or where two smaller groups combine to become a larger group. A hybrid can be a useful interim arrangement in a group working towards greater cooperation. It may, in some cases, be a more realistic model.

The hybrid model is often useful in urban contexts where two or more larger churches cooperate, each with one or more smaller churches attached to them.

At best, this model recognizes the different level of resourcing possible in larger and smaller churches. It enables them to come together and find a way forward.

At worst, this can just be a muddle, with old patterns in the two separate groupings dominating, and the churches never seeing themselves as belonging to one MPB.

Do you recognize your churches in this model?

What do you think?

These metaphors and models are intended to help you think about how things are now – but also how they could be in future. They are not intended to be taken too seriously. If you were to gather a group to discuss them, there is much fun to be had, with serious intent, when they look at these possibilities. Just thinking about them with others from across the churches is a good way to deepen relationships.

Learning to trust

Growing good, healthy relationships between individuals, leaders and congregations across an MPB takes time and demands a willingness to trust one another. The advantages, however, are many. People discover ways to help each other: praying, resourcing, sharing, doing life together, discussing, dreaming dreams and seeking God together.

At its best, this means that church communities are encouraged to know that they are not alone, and that even if their numbers are very small, they belong more widely than just to their own little church.

In the CPAS learning-community gatherings that have met over the last nine years, it has become clear that spending time in discussion with others from their MPBs, and therefore learning to trust one another, are highly valued by people.

What other ways can trusting relationships be built? You might want to try the following three.

1 Have fun

Having fun together is one of the best things you can do to deepen relationships across the group of churches. It was noticeable in the pandemic that people in some MPBs started to get to know each other better through the fun events created online. Whether onsite or online, try a range of fun things to see what works well with people of different ages and stages of life. Keep it simple but plan well, so people can genuinely relax and enjoy themselves. Quizzes, treasure hunts, online games, barn dances, bring-and-share meals, trips out … there are many possibilities. Be creative.

Of course, when you have fun events for people to join in, they are great opportunities to bring other people along who want to find out more about the churches but who are not ready to come to a service.

2 Encourage great hospitality

Great hospitality can be a vital key to helping groups of churches work well together. It does not need to be complicated, but regular gatherings for food and sharing of lives helps people live well as disciples together. If we, as church leaders, can model relaxed, welcoming hospitality towards people in both our churches and our homes, we encourage others to do the same. Of course, sensitivity to culture and safeguarding issues must be addressed. In some places, people would never invite others into their homes, so hospitality should be in church or community buildings.

Of course, these events are not about impressing people with our venues, but rather about opening our hearts and lives to people to welcome them. They are about showing the love of Jesus and his deep acceptance of people. They are about creating places of warmth and honour in a world that can be frightening and cold. They are about time generously given to share thoughts and feelings, fun and life stories. If we plan no time for hospitality, we may be missing one of the best things in the Christian life.

One vicar invited all the churchwardens from the benefice to a meal. About halfway through the evening, one warden asked what the issue was that they were there to discuss. The warden marvelled, and visibly relaxed, when the reply came that they were just there to get to know each other and enjoy time together.

It has often been said that the Christian faith is about prayer and parties. It might be a good approach to adopt. Nor does all the responsibility for hospitality have to fall to the leaders. Almost every church will have people with extraordinary gifts of hospitality. These are just the people to organize a summer picnic, or a bring-and-share winter lunch in one of your churches or church halls, or to dream up a really fun online evening together.

In the Gospels, Jesus himself was observed to be supportive of parties – though this was used as an accusation by those who were struggling to appreciate his encouragement of celebrations (Luke 5.33–39). Think of the wedding in Cana, where he supplied the best wine (John 2.1–12); his willing acceptance of Matthew's invitation to his party of restoration (Matthew 9.9–11); his happy use of fishermen's boats (Mark 4.1); or his careful preparation of the upper room (Luke 22.10–12).

In some MPBs, events put on by individual churches – charity fund-raisers, concerts, sports events, suppers and so on – are willingly and generously supported by people from the other churches. This is group hospitality in action.

3 Make use of technology

We have mentioned the opportunities that have opened up in recent years for using technology well to help people relate effectively across a group of churches. However, there may well be more that we can do. Clergy report being surprised by how many people have enthusiastically joined online prayers of various kinds – far more than would come out for a prayer meeting.

Of course, one of the glories of online events is that they can be short and sweet, allowing people to fit them into busy lives. A 20-minute Morning or Evening Prayer is easier to commit to than an hour's meeting that involves travel or childcare. Or, when working on a cross-benefice project, a short regular meeting online can keep things on track – perhaps backed up by a WhatsApp or other text-based group. We cannot afford to ignore these possibilities, especially if we are hoping to engage with younger generations for whom screen-based relating is completely normal.

Again, if our churches can use digital projection, recorded sermons can be shared across a group during services, allowing, on occasion, the whole benefice to be sharing the same content. Installing Wi-Fi allows for live streaming and even sharing of one service to another church in real time if that proves helpful.

Increasing numbers of people expect to find out about church life via a website or Facebook page or on other internet platforms, rather than a leaflet or magazine. These online options help people across a benefice to track and support what the other churches are doing, as well as providing outsiders with some initial information about what churches do. Some short videos of local people talking about what it means to them to be followers of Jesus would bring it to life.

These online ideas all involve work and investment, but the dividends could be huge. Take time with your PCCs or Group Council to review your online presence, and how well you are using technology to help your churches worship, pray, have fun and work well together. With younger people especially living so much of their lives there, the virtual world is a wide-open mission field that we can explore together. In many ways, it makes it easier to reach our communities, so make the most of the opportunities where you can.

Questions to consider

1 Can you put into a couple of sentences the reasons that you believe your group of churches – whether two or twenty – exists within the purposes of God?

2 What are your relationships like across the group? Which metaphors or models were helpful – or did you come up with better, more relevant ones?

3 How are you doing with shared fun and hospitality across your churches? What could you plan in the next few months that will bring people together? Who are the key people you know with God-given talents in hospitality?

4 Are there simple online things you could do – prayer events, social events, joint services – that might deepen your relationships across churches with minimal effort?

Story time

One benefice decided to give concentrated attention to their social media communication, using it to raise their profile and publicize events. The result was extraordinarily encouraging. The various social and hospitality-based initiatives across the churches were surprisingly well attended. A 'Christmas pudding club' attracted around 100 people; the Messy church in one community started growing; a breakfast church proved so successful in one church that another in the group decided to run one too; and yet another church decided to work with its community on becoming an eco-church, including establishing two allotments for community use.

A different benefice started a straight-from-the-book (or the app) daily Morning Prayer service online during lockdown. Not only were they surprised by the number of people who attended, and how they began to get to know each other, but they were also delighted to see people taking turns in leading the service who had never done so before.

5

Our Leaders, Part 1

Rediscovering the body of Christ

For as in one body we have many members, and not all the members have the same function, so we, who are many, are one body in Christ, and individually we are members one of another. We have gifts that differ according to the grace given to us: prophecy, in proportion to faith; ministry, in ministering; the teacher, in teaching; the exhorter, in exhortation; the giver, in generosity; the leader, in diligence; the compassionate, in cheerfulness. (Romans 12.4–8)

'I am always impressed by how strong a sense of vocation many of our lay leaders have, and how hard they work to help the churches do well.' (Quote from the coalface)

Leaders for churches

MPBs are great places for developing leaders. This chapter focuses on the challenges of recruiting and developing leaders in our churches. Obviously, many in our churches will also be leaders in their places of work and leisure, but the focus here is on church-based activities.

The body of Christ

The verses above are thrilling stuff. How marvellous to think of every follower of Jesus being given not only different gifts from God, but also the grace to use them wisely and well. Thinking about the people who are part of the churches in your group, you can probably see all of the gifts mentioned above in different people. Are some good at helping people see what God's point of view might be in a situation? They may well have prophetic gifts. Do some teach the faith to others, easily and naturally, whether formally or informally? There are your teachers. What about those who chivvy and encourage everyone along the road of faith? The exhorters. And so it goes on.

However, when we look at the culture of many of our churches around the country, we can see that people do not always realize that all of us together make up the body of Christ. Congregations tend to put clergy on a pedestal and believe that all the gifts are concentrated in them. Clergy can be complicit in such understandings. The existence of MPBs, however, challenges us to find a more biblical way of understanding God's rich gifts. Yes, there are specific things that only licensed and ordained leaders can do, but God gives everyone gifts of one kind or another. If their churches are to survive, let alone thrive, incumbents and lay leaders have to prioritize helping people to find and use their gifts. It is our responsibility to create opportunities for people to 'have a go' at new things, to discover their gifts. For example, often our church schools are better at giving children opportunities to present, write prayers and act out Bible stories than we are. A child-led or teenage-led service can be the most enormous blessing for all. Only this way may everyone grow in faith, build strong church communities and learn to share the good news of Jesus with their families, friends, colleagues and neighbours.

Ministry versus leadership

In looking at developing leaders to take responsibilities across our churches, it helps to clarify things by making a distinction between 'ministry' and 'leadership'. While there are many definitions for these, the following are based on Ian Jagelman's book *The Empowered Church: Releasing Ministry through Effective Leadership* (Port Orchard, WA: Ark House Press, 2016):

Ministry: any activity that serves the needs of people.
Ministry includes helping people grow in godliness, praying, evangelism, caring, teaching, preaching, visiting, ministering the sacraments.

Leadership: any activity that directs, influences or facilitates ministry by others.

Leadership includes training, vision, thinking, strategic planning, building teams, growing leaders, shaping culture.

In the Gospels, we see Jesus involved in both ministry and leadership. In his three years with the disciples, he started by demonstrating the works of ministry but soon showed himself to be a leader too as he trained and released his disciples into using their own God-given gifts. When the Spirit came in new ways at Pentecost, the disciples were ready to be empowered. They went out and turned the world upside down.

As church leaders, we would be wise to follow this pattern. We need to be doing the ministry ourselves to a certain extent, and to model it well; but we also need to train others to do ministry, and eventually leadership too. We want to get to the point where we are training leaders to train leaders. God has given gifts and graces generously to his children and invites us all to use them to bless others inside and outside the churches.

Christian leaders

What, then, makes a Christian leader? 'Leadership' is a contested concept in Christian circles, and there is sensible wariness about adopting wholesale leadership understandings and strategies from the world of business and corporate training. Interestingly, however, we see business training increasingly prizing – usually without realizing it – Christian values and understandings of leadership. So, for example, one of the key indicators of success for CEOs is humility – a Christian value if ever there was one. It seems that the most fruitful way forward in the midst of all the debate is to recognize four facts:

1 Both the Old and New Testaments are full of stories of people not only being called by God into positions of leadership, but also with records of their growth into godly leadership. Think of Moses learning to delegate responsibility (Exodus 18.13–26) or Peter being challenged by God to take the gospel to the Gentiles (in Acts 10).

2 Down the centuries of the Christian Church, much attention has been given to the topic of godly leadership, and much wisdom accu-

mulated: for example, Gregory the Great's treatises on the subject (*The Book of Pastoral Rule*) or the distillation of the priestly task into the questions in the ordination service.

3 There is a huge amount of useful research being done in the business world into what makes a good leader in today's culture with its continual change and challenge.

4 Many Christian leaders down the centuries have modelled godly leadership in the workplace and the marketplace.

These four facts mean that we in the churches have much to offer the rest of the world in how to develop reliable, humble, visionary leaders of integrity. It also means that there are strands of wisdom to learn from the business world, often by careful scrutiny and translation into the work of the churches. Some of the most effective thinkers in business leadership development and training are Christians whose training spans both churches and the wider market.

As we blend together the examples and stories of leaders in the Bible with the wisdom from contemporary Christian and secular research into leadership, we can help leaders at all levels in our churches to reflect on what it means to be a good and effective Christian leader. We can muse with them on how to grow in understanding and skill for their role.

There are two particular considerations for Christian leaders to look at here, whether they are leaders in churches, workplaces or both.

1 Christ-like leading – character

The first vital consideration for any sort of Christian leader is to learn from Jesus. His example is key, as are his words about leaders. Perhaps we think first about those challenging words in Matthew 20.25–28:

> But Jesus called them to him and said, 'You know that the rulers of the Gentiles lord it over them, and their great ones are tyrants over them. It will not be so among you; but whoever wishes to be great among you must be your servant, and whoever wishes to be first among you must be your slave; just as the Son of Man came not to be served but to serve, and to give his life a ransom for many.'

With this as our starting point, we realize that who we are, our character, matters at least as much as our actions as leaders. Jesus was both confident in who he was, and willing to work, serve and sacrifice for the sake of others.

The role of the Christian leader, lay and ordained, is not about status, power or invincibility, but about service, humility and daily responsiveness to the leading of the Spirit of God.

2 Christ-like leading – limitations

The second consideration, modelled by Jesus, is accepting our limitations. The fact that Jesus was sure of his identity meant that he stayed close to his Father, doing only what the Father told him (John 5.19). Jesus, like us, had human limits. He could not heal everyone, preach to everyone or be in more than one place at a time. Within those limits, he was clear about what he should do and sometimes that meant he had to say 'no' to requests. And as we recognized in Chapter 1, he prioritized prayer, needing his Father's guidance in all things. As leaders, we too need to recognize our very real limits. We only have a limited amount of time and energy. We, like Jesus, need rhythms of activity, recreation and rest.

These are matters we must bear in mind as we recruit, encourage and train others to take leadership roles in our churches and communities. We need to ensure they are not burning out or taking on too much. If that means we need to pare down our church activities, we may have to accept that. We are, all of us, called to listen to the Father as Jesus did and try our best to do only what he wants us to do.

The leaders we need

We could easily be sidetracked by the wider questions of whether we need more ordained leaders across the Church of England, more lay leaders or more of both. We could discuss endlessly how exactly they should be trained and resourced, whether upfront or as lifelong learning. Should it be separate training or on-the-job; academic or practical, or both? What, exactly, should lay leaders be allowed or not allowed to do? What precise theological, ontological and operational difference does ordination make? Are we faithful to God's call in our understanding and practices of lay and ordained leadership?

The questions are numerous, and the source of passionate and continuing debate at all levels of church life. We will probably go on discussing them for years to come.

In the meantime, however, we want our MPBs to thrive. We want to see churches that are welcoming and open-hearted, confident in showing and sharing the love of God in Christ, open to the leading of the Holy Spirit.

We want to see people growing in faith and increasingly aware of the presence of God in their day-to-day lives. We want to see the love of God being demonstrated and talked about easily, confidently and appropriately in work places, schools, colleges, retirement homes, parents' forums, online networks, social media and so on.

We want to see pastoral care done well in our churches and communities. We want to know that people are ready to offer to say a prayer with a friend in need, as well as caring for them in practical ways.

We want to see people step into the rich and varied callings of God on their lives in winsome and distinctly Christian ways. It will look different for each person. Across our churches, individuals may be called and gifted by God to, for example:

- Campaign on climate change.
- Knit prayer shawls for those going into hospital.
- Run community cafés.
- Host home groups and enquirers' events.
- Become prayer warriors.
- Share faith with children and teenagers.

In their places of work and leisure, individuals may be called and gifted by God to, for example:

- Show and share the love of Christ among their family and friends.
- Demonstrate honesty and integrity at work.
- Challenge injustices or malpractices.
- Support charities and community initiatives.
- Care for those in need.
- Become school governors.

There are endless callings and giftings from God in the lives of the faithful followers of Christ who make up our churches.

For our churches to even start becoming such visionary, fruitful places where the kingdom of God can grow, we have already acknowledged that one leader alone, the incumbent, cannot do everything needed for one church, let alone 6 or 16. Yet the patterns of generations are remarkably persistent. Just recently, I spoke with someone who had changed churches because their vicar, who was incumbent of several churches, had not been to visit when their relation – a faithful church member – was ill. Other church members had been, so the church was caring for the family, but the absence of the vicar was felt too keenly for them to remain in that benefice. These patterns have been around for generations. They are deeply rooted and hard to change.

These are tricky issues, and we need to speak about them often to enable culture change to happen. We need to be honest about what is and what is not possible for one incumbent to do.

In response to this need for more leaders, many dioceses are encouraging the development of 'focal ministers' in the MPBs in their dioceses. While different terminology exists, the underlying idea is that each individual church or new congregation or fresh expression of church needs its own identifiable leader, under the oversight of the incumbent. They may be lay or ordained, but they have the primary responsibility for that church. Where this idea has taken root successfully, churches have discovered a new impetus towards growth and mission. It also means recognition for those who have, informally, been living out such a role for years.

So we need to be raising up new leaders of all ages. Not just 'helpers', but older people, younger people and children who are discovering their God-given callings to serve and lead. Some will be ready to take on significant responsibility as church wardens or focal ministers. Others will be ready to learn to teach the faith whether to adults, children or young people.

Incumbents of MPBs also need to take advantage of diocesan or other short courses available to help orientate worship leaders, pastoral carers, youth and children's leaders, focal ministers, leaders in mission and those in other roles. Then there needs to be continued investment in those leaders into the future.

MPBs, with their multiple services and varied needs, are potentially excellent places to train up new leaders. They have so many opportunities for people to 'have a go'. What might you be looking for in developing leaders? Here are three possibilities to consider.

1 Leaders who enable

Incumbents and others who take overall responsibility in MPBs nearly always know that developing leaders is the only way forward, but struggle to do so. There are issues that we need to address head-on if overall leaders are to be genuine and effective in their vision to enable others. For a start, incumbents need to:

- Be willing to delegate power to other leaders. This is not easy to do, but clergy who insist on doing everything themselves, or micro-managing other leaders, may well suffer burnout, and are bound to discourage and frustrate their lay leaders.
- Be clear about the roles they are asking people to take on, and their parameters.
- Be intentional about ensuring new leaders have the support and help they need to inhabit their roles.
- Be willing to step back as new leaders find their feet and take more responsibility.
- Be patient and careful to continue to support and mentor leaders – perhaps in groups.
- Be ready to take personal responsibility for things that go wrong, and help leaders to recover and continue.
- Give all the credit to the relevant leaders when things go well.

Often we think that it would be easier to do things ourselves – and sometimes that is true – but as we invest in people, gradually we can release areas of ministry to them.

In return, incumbents also need to discuss their hopes of emerging leaders. Are they willing to:

- Support others across the group, even though based in their own church?

- Recognize the complexities of life for the incumbent working with multiple churches and fresh expressions of church?
- Take initiative but still be subject to the oversight of the incumbent?
- Be publicly loyal and supportive to the incumbent?
- Take issues straight to the incumbent for honest conversation rather than fomenting gossip?

2 Leaders we already have

Across the churches in any one benefice, there may well be natural leaders or those with skills from their workplace that can be shared in training others. Make the most of who you have.

You could ask them to share their experience of leading in schools, business, as union representatives, in the local community, in politics, hospitality or commerce. While not all their experiences will translate directly into church life, learning from different angles can only enrich the experience for all, and gives the opportunity to encourage budding leaders in reflective practice.

Gradually, you can build a team of leaders across the benefice who are able to think strategically and prioritize growth, rather than being overwhelmed by the relentless needs of maintenance. We will talk about good teamwork in the next chapter.

We need to invest in and support our key leaders, so that they can then invest in and support the other leaders in their churches or fresh expressions of church. Even if we are only talking tiny numbers of people to begin with, momentum can spread as people see that becoming a leader in God's Church does not mean being given a role and then being left to sink or swim; it means being part of a group of leaders all seeking God's way forward together.

3 Leaders of all ages

In Chapter 2 we talked about the changes that have occurred in recent decades in education. We noticed that children and teenagers are no longer expected to sit alone and absorb the wisdom of the teacher and learn by rote, but rather they explore topics together in groups.

So just like the uniformed organizations, which caught on to this generations ago, we need to think about what we hope for, what we provide for and what we expect of the children in our midst. Perhaps, like many others, your first experience of leadership was in Cubs, Brownies, Boys' or Girls' Brigade or another such organization – and that at a very young age.

I long for our churches to pick up on this great example. For that to happen, we have to realize the potential of children to lead, on appropriate occasions, the whole people of God. It is all too easy to see children or young people as only needing to receive, learn and wait in the wings until considered old enough to take on responsibility. However, where they are given the opportunity to lead – worship, prayers, talks, drama, sharing their faith – young people often challenge the older disciples with their clarity of thought and deep spiritual understanding.

They are also far more likely to feel that they belong, and hence to stay at church as they grow up. In addition, like any adult who leads in church life, there is no faster way to grow in their own following of Jesus than seeking to help, serve and lead others.

As you look across your churches, and perhaps church schools too, what could you do to help children and young people to grow as leaders? By giving them opportunities to lead in church, we are ourselves blessed and enable upcoming generations to grow well as disciples, as responsible people and as leaders. In MPBs we may well be in a strong position to grow young leaders, by bringing the children and young people we have together across churches to create a big enough group to try leadership activities together. Are there partnerships you can develop with a local church school? Some have child-led worship events during the week, plus those held in church at festival times. Could you give them further opportunities in church?

Teenagers especially can give so much to church life. They are often ahead of everyone in understanding and operating technology. They can plan and lead worship, given some help and encouragement. Ask older teens to join a PCC or Group Council for a year, or be part of a Messy church planning team, band or music group. We cannot afford to mark time with or sideline these young disciples. We need to treasure those we have, make space for them to grow, and be willing to change the way we do things to accommodate their ideas and hopes.

We have so much to learn from them.

Make the most of diocesan or other training

It is also worth researching and signing up emerging leaders for any diocesan leaders' training that is open to them. While some will want to explore reader ministry or ordination, many dioceses now offer short courses for licensed ministries that have one focus – pastoral, missional, youth and children or worship leading, for example. These can give confidence to those who are timid and open up opportunities for them to try new things. One of the joys of an MPB is that you can develop a team of people who will work not only in their own church but also be willing to share their gifts with other churches in the group.

Questions to consider

1 Do the people in your churches recognize themselves as gifted and graced parts of the body of Christ? If not, what can you do to help them see themselves this way?

2 How are you doing with recruiting and training leaders to different roles? What is going well and what is tricky?

3 Are you making the most of training opportunities from the diocese or from providers like CPAS? You may well want to do the downloadable Thrive course that accompanies this book or take a look at Growing Leaders or Growing Young Leaders (downloadable courses that combine teaching, mentoring and practical application, focusing on the foundation, characteristics and key skills of Christian leadership).

4 However many children and young people there are across our benefice, how are we treasuring them and helping them grow as disciples and leaders?

Story time

A retired headteacher, a lifelong follower of Christ, was invited to do a short diocesan leadership course. He completed the general training weeks and then joined a small group thinking about mission. His first excitement was in realizing that he could share his faith with a long-term golfing friend. Then he started dreaming up ideas for his own local church to reach out with God's love into their community. As it turned out, he didn't have many years left to live, but they were spent pestering his incumbent with his passion and creative ideas for mission and being an inspiring example as a leader in mission to all the churches in the benefice.

In one school that drew children from across the benefice, there was an after-school club for primary children, run jointly by adults from both school and churches. Over the course of one school term, they took 'leaders' as their theme – looking at leaders from the Bible and from history. They even invited the headteacher to come one day to talk about what it was like to lead a school. The children lapped up the topic, keen to learn. They were invited to reflect on their own leadership roles in school and elsewhere.

Some teenagers in a benefice were members of a youth project in the next town. They went to the youth club in their own church, but also went to the project once a week. In the summer, the youth project helped various churches in the area put on Christian holiday clubs for primary-aged children, providing material and support. In this one benefice, the teenagers themselves ran the holiday club for up to 70 children. There were adults involved of course, and safeguarding requirements were properly met. The adults present were there to support, oversee and advise when needed, and to pray for and with the teenagers. In the evenings, at the youth project, there were sessions for all the teenagers helping at the holiday clubs. This was a brilliant way to train up and release young leaders and it was often a highlight of their year.

6

Our Leaders, Part 2

Growing great teams

> But speaking the truth in love, we must grow up in every way into him who is the head, into Christ, from whom the whole body, joined and knitted together by every ligament with which it is equipped, as each part is working properly, promotes the body's growth in building itself up in love. (Ephesians 4.15–16)

> *'I enjoy leading a multi-parish benefice. There are great opportunities for developing the ministry and I enjoy working as part of a team.'* (Quote from the coalface)

Team experience

It is highly likely that you have been part of a team at some time in your life, probably more than once. Perhaps you have known the joy and delight of being part of a great team – one where people know and accept each other with all their strengths and weaknesses, where they support each other to do well, where they encourage, challenge and work well together. That sort of team is greater than the sum of its parts, producing significant outcomes, while team members feel privileged to belong to it.

At the other end of the scale are the terrible teams: acrimonious, argumentative, where everyone protects their own corner, their own role and their own significance. In such a team, the work is undermined continually by suspicion and animosity, and sometimes disappears altogether. People find it a bruising experience and it leaves them wary of being part of another team.

It is likely that our experience has been between those two extremes, but it helps if we are wise to the dynamics of teamwork, and the possible issues, if we are to build effective and happy teams across our benefice. Good teams across MPBs can multiply effectiveness in many ways. They can stop ordained or lay leaders feeling lonely, while also bringing new creativity and shared responsibility throughout the benefice group.

Individual church teams

Incumbents with several churches to oversee can be relieved of a great deal of stress by a small team that takes responsibility for the basics of running each church community and its buildings. That might seem like a pipe dream for those who are desperately trying to fill even the statutory roles. However, a churchwarden and a couple of others who are willing and able could be encouraged to meet together, perhaps for a quick online meeting, once a week to track such things as:

1 Those leading the various parts of services.
2 Any plans for festivals and upcoming events.
3 Urgent building and finance issues.
4 Vision for the future.

Even if there is an appointed focal leader, whether lay or ordained, they will need a team around them to support their work. A small team in each church community is a great thing to aim for, and starting to talk about it with people can open up the way for establishing such teams.

Cross-benefice teams

In other circumstances, particularly for new projects, creating cross-church teams can be hugely effective. Often, one church alone does not have the resources for mission projects, but by working together, MPBs can surprise themselves with what is possible. Some examples are:

- Gathering people together to learn how to lead different parts of services, such as intercessions, readings, testimonies, worship leading, working with different types of musicians and so on.
- Working together to set up and run a Messy church, forest church, breakfast church or similar for children and families.
- Bringing together people with a passion for the church buildings to share plans and encouragement, wisdom and knowledge.
- Working on particular social action projects or campaigns – making the most of the people across a number of churches who share a passion for particular issues.
- Running lunch clubs for the elderly or cafés for the whole community.
- Starting a youth group or fresh expression of church.

Whether a team is small or large, short or long term, official or informal, good teams are a great blessing.

Benefice vision groups

At the heart of all these things, gathering a team together across a benefice to dream dreams and try new things can often bring new life, focus and energy to a group of churches. Such a team would need to report to the PCCs or Group Council, but its remit is to think and pray about strategy. When inviting people to be part of it, it is worth looking for people who are:

- Willing to look beyond their particular patch, to think about how plans can best be made for the whole benefice.
- Able to think more long term than just managing the next crisis or reacting to the next possibility.
- Willing to be open to the big picture and the ways that the Spirit of God may be leading the benefice.
- Keen to enable others, not do everything themselves.

A team like this could work together very effectively. Care needs to be taken to ensure that DCCs, PCCs or Group Councils know that they are the ones ultimately making the decisions, but a leadership team of creative, visionary and grounded people can initiate in new ways.

Growing healthy teams

As we think about establishing and growing teams across a benefice, we need to consider what Christian teams require in order to function well. This simple picture of a flower reminds us about those various factors, and that, in all these endeavours, we are hoping, as Mother Teresa said, to do 'something beautiful for God'.

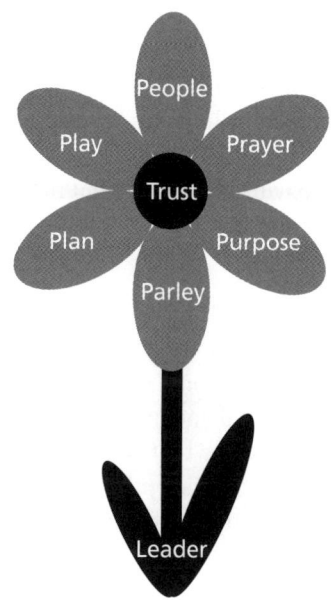

The stem of the flower represents the leader of the team, who takes overall responsibility for this group of people and their work together. As we look at each of the other factors in the growing of a healthy team, we will also highlight the particular responsibility of the team or group leader.

Prioritizing trust

If a team or group is going to get anything done well, its members need to trust one another. Trust does not happen overnight, but as people work together, share their lives and complete projects together, they learn to trust one another. All the other parts of the flower are important, but without trust there is nothing to hold the petals of the flower together.

So when bringing a team together, the leader may want to start by encouraging mutual agreement on healthy ground rules regarding how the members will work together. The following questions might help:

- What standards of behaviour are the team members going to sign up to?
- What norms will there be for meetings, like starting and ending on time, being clear about actions agreed, and who is taking notes?

- What will the team expect of each other in terms of getting things done? Can they agree to ask for help if they need it and to be honest if plans go awry?
- How will the team acknowledge people's contributions and completed actions?
- How will the team celebrate the milestones of the project?

We will also think about helping the team get to know each other in the section on play.

People

The people on a team can make or break it. There are various factors to consider if you have a choice as to who to invite on to a team – although we all know that sometimes you have to work with inherited teams or have very little option as to who to involve, especially to start with. Here are four things to consider.

Diversity

Research shows that the more diverse your team, the more creative and effective it will be. The variety of opinions and voices that come with people of different ages, genders and backgrounds make for better, more considered dreams and plans. So beware of looking just for those who will agree with the leader, or who are similar in outlook and life experience. Of course, a diverse team means you may need to work rather harder to get to know, understand and trust each other, but that is all to the good. The body of Christ is a wonderful place to be, in all its glorious range of people.

Range of skills and gifts

In subsequent sections we will think through the variety of gifts needed on a team, but note here that a range of practical and ministry skills is essential. A team of people who all have life experience of accounting may not be as effective as one with a wider range of skills and understanding. We need big-picture thinkers and careful-detail people; pastoral carers and vision casters; those who are great at group dynamics; and others who have a light touch and make people laugh.

Growing people

It's always worth looking for people who can grow into new roles and responsibilities as a result of being part of a team. I wonder who gave you your first chance to be a member of a good team?

Time-limited

There may be two anxieties about being part of a team. The first and most obvious one is that, if individuals agree to join, they will be stuck with the responsibility for endless years ahead. The other is that they will not be allowed to be on the team long enough to make a significant contribution. Therefore, setting the terms of membership from the start, and for new members joining later on, is both fair and realistic.

Once again, it is the leader of the team's responsibility to ensure that these things are taken into consideration.

Prayer

Although it may seem obvious, any effective team in an MPB is one that grounds all that it does in learning to pray together. It recognizes its identity as a Christian team and as part of the body of Christ. Wholesale and uncritical adoption of attitudes and practices that may have been part of the members' work or community teams may not be appropriate. To do the work of God well, the team must set praying about it as its top priority, both together and individually.

We need all the wisdom that comes from God in growing our churches and fresh expressions across a benefice, and the way we come to that godly wisdom is by taking our praying and engagement with Scripture seriously. So whatever language and style works for your situation, do ensure that you do just that.

In addition, you may even have people in the team who are gifted intercessors, so ask them to pray specifically for the current vision or project.

Whoever leads the team must model this commitment to prayer:

- Surrendering the whole project to God.
- Praying for it, within and beyond the meetings.
- Modelling the use of the *Thrive Prayer Guide*.

Purpose

From the start or the relaunch of a team, it matters that its purpose is clear, even if that is 'discerning vision for the future'. Be specific about the central task and ensure that everyone is on board with that. Whether the group is intended to be long-lasting or to deliver a specific time-bound project, the terms of engagement need to be clear to everyone.

People's time is precious, increasingly so. We do not want to annoy or exhaust people with unnecessarily long or unfocused meetings. Think clearly about how often you need to meet, for how long, and whether that always needs to be onsite, or can sometimes be online in order to save people travelling – especially for large cross-benefice groups. Start on time, every time and – crucially – finish on time.

The team leader is obviously responsible for setting these parameters and agreeing the purpose of the group with everyone. If you are not a task-focused person yourself, and struggle to keep things on message, make sure you work with someone who is and give them appropriate responsibility.

Parley

This is a slightly awkward word – to fit with all the P words – for learning to deal with the inevitable awkward moments in a team. A team can only grow in effectiveness when it learns to do disagreement and conflict well.

When you take care to hear everyone's voice and opinion in a discussion, it will not be long before disagreement arises. This is a good thing. Many people shy away from conflict, and Christians can especially assume that they need to be 'nice' on all occasions and smooth over differing points of view. However, when we push disagreement underground it comes out in different ways, and people may become obstructive or reluctant when it is time to act on decisions made, because their viewpoints were not considered properly in the process.

Therefore, discuss together as a team how you are going to handle disagreement well. Good disagreement is always about the issues involved. Good disagreement does not accuse people nor behave rudely. Bad disagreement is personal and unkind. It involves accusation and fear.

To achieve good disagreement, the team needs to agree its behavioural norms and then the leader needs to be willing to:

- Call out bad behaviour.
- Be called out themselves if they overstep the boundaries of good disagreement.
- Ensure that everyone has a chance to express their thoughts.
- Encourage robust and respectful discussion.

Plan

Once you have an established purpose, it is time to make a plan. Obviously, as we have already said, seeking God's will in all of this is a vital part of the process. Then, together, be very practical about how the project is going to move forward.

Agree the actions and what order they will come in, and then work out who the best people are to take those actions. Putting a deadline on those actions will make them more likely to happen. Playing to people's strengths is a good principle to have at the forefront here. For example, catering for an event would cause many people great joy but others to have sleepless nights. The same is true for standing up in front of people to enthuse them about a project or dealing with a long list of detailed administrative tasks.

Between meetings, find a way of keeping tabs on how people are getting on with their commitments, which is easier if you have already agreed to help each other out with tasks. Some groups will work well with an online task tracker that they all use.

If yours is a long or complex project, keep revisiting it and revising it in your meetings – though always keeping the larger purpose in mind so that you are not distracted by seemingly good ideas that will actually take you off course.

Play

This rather surprising title underlines the need for teams to get to know one another and share life together. For those who are particularly task-focused, the thought of 'wasting time' on shared food and drinks together, or taking time out to do more social things, might seem rather annoying. It is as we share the normal ups and downs of life, however, as well as the team's tasks, that our trust in one another grows.

Give some freedom to the team members who are great at group dynamics to make the most of the chances for chat, sharing, vulnerability and fun. This might be as small as each person giving a one-minute update on their own news at the start of the meeting, or as ambitious as planning an annual summer meal for the team.

Surely those young men and women who became Jesus' close group of disciples – sharing life day-to-day with him, learning from him, providing for him and so on – gave up their lives to be with him not just because of the vision he gave them, but because they loved his company? Surely there was fun and laughter, play and delight along the road between the villages and towns that Jesus and his disciples visited, as well as the serious discussion, questioning and learning that we see in Scripture?

Our churches are more likely to grow when we show ourselves to be people of joy. A quick internet search for Bible verses about joy and rejoicing will reveal hundreds of them. As we rejoice with delight in the presence of God, as we rejoice with delight in each other, we deepen our faith and our relationships and God fills us with energy for the task of spreading the love of Christ.

Great teams

Well-functioning teams enable members to delight in their work and be willing to give of their time and energy to further the projects they are pursuing. It is more than worth putting in the effort to create and develop great teams.

Questions to consider

1 Reflect on your experience of teams – in various settings. What have you learned along the way about the blessings and challenges of working in teams?

2 If you already have teams across your benefice, how are they going? How might they be encouraged to work together more effectively?

3 As you think about the flower diagram, does it make sense for you? Is there anything missing? How might it be of help to you?

4 What could you do today that will increase your delight in life and your experience of the joy of God's love?

Story time

One group of rural churches, in response to this need to recruit, train, support and encourage new leaders across the benefice, created a monthly evening gathering specifically for anyone who had leadership responsibility in any of the churches in the benefice. It was in a different church community each month, held in the church or community hall if there was one, with a bring-and-share meal. After food and the chance for people to get to know each other, there was worship, then some sort of input – whether from an outside speaker, one of the clergy, or a film to watch, followed by discussion in groups. It proved to be a lively, joyful and encouraging evening and anyone with leadership responsibility wanted to be there. Gradually the leaders from various teams across the benefice learned to work well together, to be distinctly Christian leaders, to support leadership across the whole benefice, and to have fun together. The incumbent said it took some organizing but was more than worth it for the fruit that it bore.

7

Our Disciples, Part 1

Being disciples

And Jesus came and said to them, 'All authority in heaven and on earth has been given to me. Go therefore and make disciples of all nations, baptizing them in the name of the Father and of the Son and of the Holy Spirit, and teaching them to obey everything I have commanded you. And remember, I am with you always, to the end of the age.' (Matthew 28.18–20)

'*It is amazing seeing people discovering gifts they didn't know they had and growing in confidence as world-changers, even in the smallest churches.*' (Quote from the coalface)

Questions about disciples

This and the following chapter focus on helping others to *become* disciples and *grow* as disciples. In this chapter we make the case for being disciples – suggesting ways to help people across our churches explore the *why* and *what* questions. Chapter 8 concentrates on *how*, looking at some disciplines of the Christian life.

Holy moments

The elderly lady was part of a PCC evening discussing the work of the benefice. They were meeting in a pub and had eaten a wonderful meal. The atmosphere was easy, relaxed. The core group gave a short presentation on what they were learning about working well together across an MPB. Then there was the chance for discussion around tables. The final section of the evening was answering questions all together again. The first question was: 'Why do you come to church?'

After a while, the lady raised her hand. 'I come to church,' she said slowly, 'to meet with God and with my friends'. There was a hush in the room. It felt like a holy moment, as if something really important had been revealed. The leader asked, 'Is this the first time you have put that into words?'

'Yes,' the lady said. 'I've been coming to church all my life but this is the first time I've thought about this and said it.'

Missed opportunity

I wonder how many faithful servants of God there are in our churches who have been coming to church all their lives, or for many years, but have never had the opportunity, the encouragement or perhaps even the language to talk about what it all means to them?

If so, we are missing out on those holy moments of sharing. We are missing out on learning from each other as fellow Christians, and our churches may even be limited to upfront ministry as their only source of information for help with their spiritual life. This is perhaps a comfortable state of affairs – we don't have to examine our lives too closely or be accountable to each other in any way – but it also leaves us all impoverished.

It may even be possible that some faithful, regular people in our churches do not even consider that they *are* disciples of Jesus. They think of themselves as church attenders but have no expectation that their faith can change and grow over time, their relationship with God deepen and his work in their lives become increasingly fruitful.

One church leader tells of taking an all-age service in one of their fairly traditional churches. They took in a flip-chart. As part of the talk, they invited the congregation to chat to those around them about some questions on the Lectionary passage of the day. The answers were written up on the flip-chart. They were wide-ranging and fascinating. After the service, the church warden said, eyes sparkling, 'I've never done anything like that before. It was *so* interesting.' Having come to faith years before at a Billy Graham event, he had not had the chance to discuss a Bible passage with others since.

Moving from being churches full of attenders to churches full of growing disciples is not an instant journey. But it can be done. In gentle steps.

Our starting point is that, whether we have 6 or 60 people in a church, and 60 or 600 people across our benefice congregations, every single individual is precious to God and is invited to know him better. Or, in the words of the prayer attributed to Richard of Chichester (in contemporary language):

> Thanks be to you, my Lord Jesus for all the benefits you have
>   given me,
> for all the pains and insults you have borne for me.
> O most merciful Redeemer, Friend, and Brother,
> of you three things I pray:
> To see you more clearly,
> love you more dearly,
> follow you more nearly,
> day by day.

The starting place

As we explore being disciples of Jesus with our congregations, it might be good to remind them of some of the basics. We might want to talk about the foundations and motivation for both evangelism and discipleship in the Great Commandments and the Great Commission.

The Great Commandments we will look at in more detail in the next chapter. But we might want to remind people that they come from the Old Testament (Deuteronomy 6.5) and were then reiterated by Jesus: 'You shall love the Lord your God with all your heart and with all your soul and with all your mind and with all your strength ... You shall love your neighbour as yourself' (Mark 12.30–31 ESV).

We can review the Christian understanding that we have not a hope of keeping these Commandments in our own strength, but that because Jesus has opened the way for us to 'approach God with freedom and confidence' (Ephesians 3.12 NIV), and because he fills us with his Spirit, we can start on the journey of learning to love God with all that we are and with all that he has given us.

Here we consider how we might examine with the people across our churches the importance of the Great Commission from Matthew 28, where Jesus instructed his disciples: 'Go therefore and make disciples of all nations, baptizing them in the name of the Father and of the Son and of the Holy Spirit, and teaching them to obey everything that I have commanded you' (Matthew 28.18–20).

As a stone dropped into a pool causes ripples to spread, the news of the gospel was to go out to 'Jerusalem, in all Judea and Samaria, and to the ends of the earth' (Acts 1.8). The disciples were to tell people the full story of Jesus and his love, to baptize them and to *teach them all that Jesus had taught them* (Matthew 28.20). They were not just to share the gospel, but to help people become *disciples.*

Faithful people in our churches may not yet have grasped that this Great Commission is just as relevant to us today, not just for lay and clergy leaders, but for everyone. We may need to remind people of the truth that our churches only grow when people of all ages are encountering Jesus.

Framing the Great Commission

We may also need to remind everyone of the extraordinary things Jesus said just before and after the Great Commission, which frame it in a powerful way. In the preceding verse he said: 'All authority in heaven and on earth has been given to me' (Matthew 28.18). There is nothing we face in our lives that is greater than the authority of Jesus. There is nothing happening in the world that leaves him puzzled or afraid. The Lord we follow is Lord indeed.

At the end of the Commission, Jesus said: 'And remember, I am with you always, to the end of the age' (Matthew 28.20). Once again, this puts us in a very strong position as we seek to help people come to faith and then grow in faith. Jesus is with us at every stage, in every invitation, in every attempt to share our faith, every effort to help people grow, every prayer prayed for others and every hesitant or confident conversation.

We may need to explain again that being witnesses to Jesus was never just about telling people and baptizing them, but always about teaching them the faith too: helping people to obey all that Jesus commands.

Could we consider at a PCC or open meeting whether we are shaping the life and activity of our churches around the Great Commandments and the Great Commission? If not, how can we begin to do so? If we are, how can we do it more effectively?

But how can we find time to do this?

Making the time to explore what it means to grow disciples with the people in our churches is a huge challenge. It may involve trying to get beyond all the competing demands of day-to-day ministry, to find energy and space to consider these things deeply with everyone and begin to initiate culture change. It may need hard-headed determination to put aside some protected time for lay and ordained leaders to plan and pray together, rather than drowning under the needs of occasional offices, multiple buildings, financial struggles and trying to find enough people to take on roles and responsibilities.

However, we remind ourselves and others that Jesus made growing disciples a huge priority. There is much to learn from the way he called his disciples and helped them mature in faith in the course of the Gospels and Acts. Part of our role has to be helping those in our churches to look at the Great Commandments and the Great Commission and to consider how Jesus lived them out – modelling discipleship for his followers. Before thinking about that, however, let's consider what a disciple might look like today.

What is a disciple?

It can be helpful to tease out with our churches what being disciples of Jesus Christ may look like in the twenty-first century. We could start with a definition taken from a dictionary. How about this one from the *Oxford English Dictionary*? A disciple is: 'A person who follows or attends upon another in order to learn from him or her; a pupil; a follower.'

In a group session across a benefice, we could list together the concepts that the word 'disciple' conjures up for us. Many people, perhaps, feel that they are unworthy to be labelled 'disciple'. But when we talk about being a disciple as being a learner, a follower, it becomes less alarming. We do not immediately have to be the kinds of people we see in the book of Acts, or the ones we know from the stories of the saints down the ages. We just have to be willing to learn, and to change, as we get to know God better. It is a journey we are all on together, and often the people who are newest to it, or who are youngest in age, have a great deal to teach those of us who have been followers of Jesus for a long time.

The following quote, from the writings of Dietrich Bonhoeffer, challenges our thinking about being disciples: 'Christianity without discipleship is always Christianity without Christ' (Dietrich Bonhoeffer, *The Cost of Discipleship*, London: SCM Press, 1989, p. 50). Our congregations cannot follow God's ways for their lives in just an hour a week in church. They need to be exploring the life of a disciple for themselves, every day, appropriate to their age and stage. As lay and ordained leaders, we need to model this in our own lives too, of course, as well as teaching, preaching and encouraging our church members along the way.

Make it visual

We can help people think about what a contemporary disciple looks like by drawing an outline of a person on a large sheet of paper and writing on the sheet the attributes of a disciple they believe to be important. Perhaps they could think of Christians they have met who have inspired them. What is it about those people's lives that shows they are followers of Jesus?

The resulting attributes usually fit into three categories:

1　*Disciplines*. Although they do not show off about their routines, somehow observers can tell that these Christians are people who are committed to habits of private prayer, engaging with the Bible, listening to God, giving generously and serving others.

2　*Character*. Often the disciples whom people are inspired by and want to emulate are great people to be around. They are trustworthy and often joyful, they are curious about things and interesting to talk to.

They are the types of people who make you feel better about being yourself, about God's good purposes in the world, about God's love for you – even without saying anything about God at all. They display the fruits of the Spirit found in Galatians 5.22–23.

3 *Surrendered*. Observers can also see that these people are surrendered to and obedient to the will of God. They can pray, 'Your kingdom come. Your will be done' (Matthew 6.10) and mean it. Even when life is very hard, or they are very afraid, they aim to stay close to God in all things. They are often people who delight in the small things of life and notice the many blessings of God that come to us all day by day.

Encouraging church members to talk with each other about what a disciple might look like encourages everyone in their own walk of faith. And always, we need to stress that our example is actually Jesus. Whether church leaders or congregation, we are not supposed to look just like another disciple, but to become the disciple of Jesus that he created each of us to be. Just look at those first disciples of Jesus – men and women so very different from each other, but all open to the work of God in their lives, learning to love and work with each other.

The example of Jesus

We could help people see what being disciples can look like by studying an early encounter Jesus had. In John 1.35–42, John the Baptist points to Jesus as he walks by, describing him to two of his own disciples as 'the Lamb of God'. The two leave John and start, literally, to follow Jesus. When Jesus turns around and sees them following, he asks what they are looking for. They ask, 'Rabbi, where are you staying?' Jesus' response is to invite them into his life. 'Come and see,' he says, and they do. But it is the two things that happen next that are so moving:

1 The narrative says that 'they remained with him that day' (John 1.39). Having found Jesus, they wanted to stay with him.

2 When they did go away, Andrew's first action was to find his brother, Simon Peter, and bring him to Jesus.

This is a great picture of what it is like to discover Jesus – both then and now. When we meet him, we want to spend time with him and we want our friends and family to know him too. There is a freshness and candour here that perhaps seem simplistic to those of us who have been leading churches and navigating their complexities over the years, but it does us no harm to remind ourselves of what is at the heart of it all – becoming disciples ourselves and introducing others to Jesus. Living out the Great Commandments *and* the Great Commission.

Of course, the story doesn't end there. Throughout the rest of the Gospels, we see Jesus demonstrating to his disciples what it looked like to follow him. The disciples watched Jesus preach, they saw him invite other people to be followers, and to 'fish for people' (Matthew 4.19). They saw him demonstrate the power of God's kingdom in miracles and healings. They saw his encounters with individuals and the way that he had something different and personal to say to each one. They heard him tell tantalizing stories about the kingdom of God, stories that stayed with them (as they stay with us) – puzzling, challenging and changing them.

The disciples had private conversations with Jesus about the meanings of his public teaching. They asked questions and tried things out. They felt his rebuke when they, like us, completely missed the point. They saw him get up early often and go away to pray. They saw him set a course of action and then follow it, even when it was unpopular with the crowds. Then the day came when they were sent out by him on their own mission trips to preach, to accept hospitality, to heal and to prepare the way for Jesus. They were starting to do the things he did. They were discovering that intimacy with God is not sufficient in itself, but that it should lead to action.

Then they saw the cost to Jesus of living in a completely different way and suffered extraordinary heartbreak as they witnessed events and people conspiring against him. However, as we see so clearly with hindsight, after the Resurrection and Ascension, after the coming of the Spirit, they were ready to speak his words and do his works, because he had trained them well as disciples. They were ready to live sacrificially as they had seen Jesus live. And some of them would die sacrificially like Jesus too.

Godly character

As we too seek to follow Jesus, and encourage those in our churches to do so too, in all the joys, struggles and sometimes tragedies of life, we need to trust that God is growing godliness in us. We often cannot see it ourselves, but others can. Just as the mustard-seed parable speaks of the tiniest of seeds growing into a tree that gives shelter to the birds, so our tiny steps of obedience and seeking God enable us to grow, so we can be a blessing to more people.

As leaders, we need to learn, and teach others, how to hear God's voice, embrace the fruits of the Spirit – love, joy, peace, patience, kindness, goodness, gentleness, faithfulness and self-control (Galatians 5.22–23) – and grow more like Jesus. Together, we discover the all-encompassing nature of God's love for us, the treasures to be found in drawing close to him and the depth of the forgiveness and healing he gives us, and we are transformed 'from glory to glory', as Paul described it (2 Corinthians 3.18 NKJV).

Variety

One of the many delights of MPBs is the potential of cross-benefice groups. These can yield a rich variety of understandings of Christian faith, which may well have a much wider range of perspectives than in a church with a more monochrome culture. The gatherings could be quite lively – and certainly help people to work out what the foundations are that they hold in common and what things are secondary issues on which they can agree to disagree.

In the next chapter we will look in more detail at the different disciplines that we can explore with people in our churches to help them grow as disciples.

Questions to consider

1 If you review the churches in your benefice, where do you see people who understand that they are disciples of Jesus and live that out each day? How can you encourage those people?

2 Where do you see people not quite aware of what being a disciple might mean? How can you start teaching and talking about the possibilities open to them?

3 What most inspires you about the example of Jesus as he taught his disciples and helped them to grow?

4 How might you pray for growth in discipleship for the people across your churches?

Story time

One MPB decided to have its own prayer commitment. They produced a sheet of simple prayers, divided into four different times of day and always including the Lord's Prayer. They invited people to take the sheets home and start using them. Just a simple step towards helping people to pray.

One group created a prayer tent – full of creative prayer activities – that was pitched in a different community across the MPB each week during the summer. People signed up for an hour's visit to the tent, to engage with the prayer activities and pray for their communities and churches, as well as for themselves, their family and friends and the needs of the world.

8

Our Disciples, Part 2

Becoming lifelong disciples together

One of the teachers of the law came and heard them debating. Noticing that Jesus had given them a good answer, he asked him, 'Of all the commandments, which is the most important?' 'The most important one,' answered Jesus, 'is this: "Hear, O Israel: the Lord our God, the Lord is one. Love the Lord your God with all your heart and with all your soul and with all your mind and with all your strength." The second is this: "Love your neighbour as yourself." There is no commandment greater than these.' (Mark 12.28–31 NIV)

'Praying the offices with people regularly in the different churches, and looking out for God's presence in what went on in those very different churches and communities, as well as delighting in the countryside in all the journeying around the benefice, sustained me.' (Quote from the coalface)

Reflecting on our own lives

We cannot help others to grow as disciples unless we are going deeper with God ourselves. The invitation is there – through the good times and the terrible times. Always, the Father loves us. Always, Jesus guides us. Always, the Spirit is with us, even if it does not feel like it. Our responsibility is to live in the truth of that, day by day, hour by hour, minute by minute. As church leaders, it is our responsibility to model the Christ-centred life that we long for everyone to have. We know this, of course, and yet it is so easy to lose sight of actually doing it.

It is in the presence of God, listening to his voice – looking out for his work in us and around us day after day, in the big things and tiny detail of life – it is in these disciplines of prayer and attention that we find the hope and vision to sustain us in the challenges of life in an MPB. The glory of situations that we know to be beyond us – like working across multiple churches – is that we are forced to seek God and his strength. We cannot buy into an illusion of self-sufficiency because the task is too big and too complex. Only working together with others and being immensely prayerful will enable us to be effective in our leading of several churches.

Our first priority

> Are the leaders of the future truly men and women of God, people with an ardent desire to dwell in God's presence, to listen to God's voice, to look at God's beauty, to touch God's incarnate Word and to taste fully God's infinite goodness?
> (Henri J. M. Nouwen, *In The Name of Jesus: Reflections on Christian Leadership*, New York: Crossroad, 1989, p. 43)

It is worth stopping and reading this quotation through slowly. Then again, and again.

It is a quote that can be both challenging and deeply refreshing. It reminds us what Christian faith is all about. It puts things the right way up. It keeps the main thing the main thing. At a time when the global challenges come thick and fast, it reminds us that our lives are given to God. He is our direction and our destination. He is our safety and our strength. Each of us can know that our life is 'hidden with Christ in God' (Colossians 3.3) and, at the same time, we can also know the truth of 'Christ in you, the hope of glory' (Colossians 1.27).

You could reflect on this quote from Henri Nouwen with others. You could ask:

- What do I think as I read these words?
- What Bible verses or stories come to mind?
- How does this quote colour my view of Jesus' prayer habits: getting up early to pray, insisting on time alone, taking a whole night to pray seeking his Father's will about who to call as his close disciples?

The Great Commandments

Having looked at the Great Commission, the quote above can lead us into helping others to then consider the Great Commandments of Jesus. For some in our churches, this might be the first time they have thought about them. For others, this might be revision. But they are the foundation of being disciples and we need our churches to engage with them. The following is one way of thinking about the Great Commandments that you might want to use with others, either as it is or adapted for your context.

1 The first commandment is to love God with our heart, mind, soul and strength

There is so much in the world of self-help and therapy about paying attention to every area of your life – your emotional, mental, spiritual and physical health. There is a great deal of wisdom in that advice, but it falls far short of the ideal. God was way ahead of the game when he gave this commandment in Deuteronomy. Jesus repeated it. Its focus is entirely different from the world's version. Instead of only looking within, absorbed with our own needs, we direct our attention to God. In determining, day by day, to love him with all of our being, we find healing along the way.

We love him with all our heart

We can see this as giving our emotional life and our will to God. We can pray: 'Let me love you today, Lord, through all the ups and downs of the day, through regularly bringing myself back to the place where I pray, "*Your* kingdom come. *Your* will be done"' (Matthew 6.10). We can do this by acknowledging our varied emotional reactions to life events, and bringing them before God. We can consciously worship God in the midst of all our daily activities.

We love him with all our mind

At the start of each day, we can give to God all the things that will occupy our mind that day. All our thinking and working and pondering. All our hopes and concerns. We can fill our minds with Scripture and learn of God's ways – even in the context of very demanding days. Will we rejoice in and be grateful for the ability to think and research, to ponder and decide, to reflect and choose? Will we be discerning in what we fill our minds with? Will we love him with all our mind?

We love him with all our soul

Here we bring our deepest needs and longings to God, asking that we may love him from the core of our being, that our whole direction in life will be a journey into the heart of God: Father, Son and Holy Spirit. That we will be like the psalmist who prayed, 'As a deer longs for flowing streams, so my soul longs for you, O God. My soul thirsts for God, for the living God' (Psalm 42.1–2).

We love him with all our strength

This puts a whole new slant on the need to exercise, eat well and rest well. Our bodies are 'temple[s] of the Holy Spirit' (1 Corinthians 6.19) and we honour and love God when we look after them properly. This is often easier said than done. Sometimes we need help from others to get ourselves on track and then keep us there. Perhaps the prayer is, 'Lord, help me to love you with my body today, with all its strengths and weaknesses, for I know "I am fearfully and wonderfully made"' (Psalm 139.14). Do we dare encourage each other to face our health issues – weight, exercise, addictions, eating or drinking too much or too little? None of this is easy stuff and our society is rife with confusing advice. Our starting point, however, is wanting to love God with all our strength – this is where we find the motivation to live well in a world full of temptations to live unhealthily or obsessively.

2 The second Commandment is to 'love your neighbour as yourself'

This commandment is a challenge to us all. Jesus' disciples were a mixed bunch of people, but Jesus consistently taught them to love one another. Even in the early Church, that proved challenging. Think of Paul and Barnabas falling out (Acts 15.36–41) or Paul imploring Euodia and Syntyche to make up in his letter to the Philippians (4.2–3). Think of the council in Jerusalem trying to work out what to do about the Gentiles and circumcision in Acts 15.

It is encouraging to remember that the early disciples sometimes struggled to love their sisters and brothers in Christ, as we can do. And yet the command of Jesus does not change: 'Love your neighbour as yourself.' We know how powerful it is when we receive the love and forgiveness of Christ from other disciples as we muddle along together in our churches. We want to do the same. Perhaps we could take time in our churches to learn about this together – talking about disciplines of forgiveness, grace and gratitude.

However, this commandment can also trip us up. For some, the interpretation of this is always to put others first, to ignore our own legitimate needs and to attempt to please others all the time. We forget that we are commanded to love our neighbour *as we love ourselves*, that loving ourselves is as much part of the Commandment as loving our neighbour. We find that hard to believe. However, if the Father himself loves us (see John 16.27, for example), surely we can love ourselves too? Humility is knowing that we are sinners saved by grace (Ephesians 2.8). Loved and forgiven.

For some, the 'as yourself' bit is hard because they have such a damaged and critical attitude towards themselves that they would never want to treat others that harshly. However, we have such good and beautiful news here. 'While we were still sinners, Christ died for us' (Romans 5.8). God knows us intimately and, as we spend time with him each day, learning to live more and more of our lives with him, his love for us begins to heal our perspective. We are increasingly free to love others as ourselves because, in Christ, we learn to love the person God has made *us* to be.

Jesus, the most sacrificial person who ever lived, took time and space for his own needs, for prayer, for rest, for refreshment, and for time with

his closest disciples. Although he was massively in demand, he prioritized his Father's call on his life. He embodied these Commandments.
He kept his focus, accepted the limitations of what was possible in three
short years – and left the results to God.

What helps you?

Having talked with our churches about ways the Great Commandments
can help us shape our lives, we can then help people consider how to live
them out. Here are some examples of ways that people pray and pursue
intimacy with God. We could consider these for ourselves and others
(and add more ideas too).

- Praying the Daily Offices.
- Times of silence and stillness – to think, pray and read the Bible.
- Lively worship with a good mix of contemporary songs and trad-
  itional hymns.
- Walking outside or playing sport.
- Academic study of the Bible and theology.
- Practical involvement in acts of care and compassion.
- Using imagination to enter into a Bible story.
- Praying with others in pairs or small groups.
- Sharing in the Eucharist.
- Using symbols and words – candles, liturgy, icons, photos, websites,
  podcasts ...
- Praying while pursuing a creative hobby.
- Praying in languages inspired by the Holy Spirit.
- Something different ...

Enjoying variety

As people share the range of things they find helpful, we can encourage
them to take the list seriously, for three reasons:

1 To realize that there are many different ways to worship God, express
   our love for him and recognize his presence. We need to be wary of
   criticizing the preferences of others or ridiculing their style. Other

people's ways of worshipping God and following Jesus are to be respected.

2 To pray to our strengths. Having helped people decide which ways of engaging with God are most helpful to them, go on to consider how to develop them further. Encourage all to make disciplined time and space available for them.

3 To encourage us to try new things. One person described doodling the name of someone she wanted to pray for, decorating around the name as she brought their needs before God. Another loved driving alone in the car, making up spontaneous songs of praise to God, safe from being overheard. Yet another said they prayed best while doing housework or gardening. What new things could your church members try?

Exploring new things together

Wonderfully, we live in an age when there is much freedom to learn new things from people of differing church backgrounds, which can only enrich our lives. What might you, across your churches, explore together? After all, these days you can find, for example:

- Charismatics going on silent retreats.
- Academic theologians discovering the lives of the mystics and saints.
- Contemplatives exploring the gifts of the Holy Spirit.
- Those from free-church backgrounds finding new treasures in the rhythms and depths of liturgy.

Of course, a good starting place will be in our own MPB. We may well have differing ways of encountering God favoured by different churches – liturgical in one place, informal in another, contemplative elsewhere and sacramental in yet another place. Encourage people to experience each other's styles of worship. Ask people to explain what different approaches mean and why they find them helpful. Winkle people out of their silos and into friendly encounter and sharing. Enjoy each other and learn from each other.

We might also want to encourage groups from our churches to explore outside our MPB. Why not visit a large town-centre church or attend a Christian festival together? Why not go to Walsingham or explore a nearby cathedral as an act of pilgrimage? Why not explore a variety of styles of online worship or listen to a series of podcasts in a small group together?

Five disciplines

As we explore disciplines of Christian life, let us look at five in more detail. Although we may already know these things, helping people revisit them throughout their lives can be rewarding and transformative.

1 Regular praying

This needs to be a topic we revisit with our congregations regularly. We have looked at it in various ways in this chapter and Chapter 2, 'Our Praying', but it goes at the top of the list.

2 Fasting and retreating

As we mentioned in the chapter on prayer, we cannot talk about prayer without thinking about sacrifices we may want to make to go deeper with God. That may be learning to fast, carefully, from food, or giving up an activity in order to free up space and energy to pray. We need these things to become a normal part of being disciples of Jesus across our churches.

For example, if you have a particular prayer concern across your churches – perhaps a world issue or a crisis more locally – wouldn't it be marvellous if people thought it normal for those who can safely do so to miss a meal in order to pray? Or if the churches decided to have an annual retreat or weekend away together to seek God and his purposes – even if, for cost purposes, that became a weekend hosted in one of your churches?

There are so many possibilities here, but if we do not plan for ways to help the people in our churches to grow in faith in corporate settings, we are not helping them to grow in their own disciplines of faith.

3 Engaging with the Bible

We also need to be helping people to get to grips with the Bible. For both new Christians and seasoned worshippers, the Bible can seem rather overwhelming. One of its wonders is that it keeps some of the cleverest minds on the planet wondering and studying, and yet its core message is simple enough for a small child to understand. We need to remind people that their reading of the Bible is a lifetime project and they only need to get to know it gradually.

Recommend Bible reading aids, apps, devotionals and group resources. Remind people that reading or listening to the Bible every day is usually about 'formation' rather than dramatic encounters with God. Just as food nourishes our bodies, so absorbing the Scriptures nourishes our souls. Our attitudes are changed over time, almost imperceptibly, as we take in more of God's character, more of God's story with the people he has made.

As well as teaching and preaching, provide opportunities for church members to share experiences and stories of reading the Bible and discovering God speaking to them through it – of being challenged about their assumptions about life and faith, or finding guidance, or discovering more about God and how to know him and follow him.

4 Church and sacraments

Another discipline that is vital to Christian growth is being part of the services and life of the churches. This is obvious to us as leaders, but in days when, for some people, regular church attendance means once or twice a month, partly because of the complexities of contemporary life, we may need to encourage them to come as often as possible. We need to model and teach how good and helpful weekly gathering can be.

That might mean Sunday or a different day. It might mean a traditional service or being part of a church plant or fresh expression. In addition it could well mean being part of a small group, prayer group, nurture course, action team or some other safe context in which to grow and to serve.

Likewise, teaching and encouraging the value of receiving the sacraments of bread and wine regularly matters. Whatever language is used

– Mass, Holy Communion, the Lord's Supper – it is a core discipline and one of the greatest blessings of church life. In an MPB, it is not always possible to provide communion for every church every week. That may mean lay leaders learning to plan and deliver Services of the Word. It certainly also means encouraging people to treasure the opportunities to receive bread and wine that *do* exist.

5 Serving and speaking

Jesus encouraged his disciples not just to cultivate a relationship with God, but to live out, speak about and demonstrate their faith in every area of their lives. It is as people take on responsibilities, start sharing their faith with others, see their prayers answered, tell their story of coming to faith, offer to pray for or with someone, or share stories of God at work in their daily lives, that faith develops. It is hard *not* to grow in your own faith when you have to study a Bible passage to talk about with children; or when you are planning an evangelistic event with others. We all grow by living it out, by taking risks and by trying new things.

Finding as many opportunities as possible for children and young people to contribute is vital. Depending on your style of church, can you train them as servers, choristers, young preachers, sidespeople, leaders in children's work, public intercessors, evangelists, service leaders and so on? Their faith will grow as they too take risks for God.

Discipline and grace

And yet, and yet … we do not want to make rods for people's backs. We need to encourage everyone to keep hold of grace. We remind our churches that these practices, and others recommended by the saints down the ages, are to help us as disciples, not achievements we need to mark up or things we need to 'get done'. Sometimes people are so paralysed by a sense of failure about regular spiritual disciplines that they give up on them. That is why we remind everyone to:

1 Find the ways of engaging honestly and openly with God and the Bible that work for them in this season of their lives.

2 Remember that, like any other discipline, these things take time to establish and will become easier as they practise.

3 Realize that the more someone spends time with Jesus, the more they will want to do so, and it will become normal to pray through the whole of their days. Other spiritual disciplines may well come more readily to us as the years go by.

4 Remember that God plays a long game and is very patient with each of his followers. Learning to pray and live like Jesus is a lifetime commitment.

Clearly, the five disciplines explored here are not an exhaustive list. However, as we encourage people to pray regularly, fast and retreat, engage with the Bible, be faithful in church attendance and receiving the sacraments, serve and tell their stories of faith, we need to be both challenging and gracious.

Disciples of all ages

As we take on board the need to grow disciples of all ages, or revisit the subject, be adventurous with how you do this. For example, the youngest can challenge the older saints with their clarity of vision and faith-filled attitudes; while the older saints can demonstrate faithfulness, perseverance and openness to the things of God to younger people.

Often, of course, the cry goes up that there are not enough people to help children and young people grow as disciples. However, here again MPBs have an advantage as their churches can work together to find motivated members for work with children and young people, in nurture groups, Messy church, café churches, Open the Book teams and so on.

They can support parents too, in living out their faith day by day at home, perhaps recommending resources for families to use, such as Parenting for Faith (www.parentingforfaith.brf.org.uk) or Raising Faith (cff.org.uk).

Across an MPB, you may only have a handful of families, but getting together to do a course like this could well be the start of a new home group, new Messy church or baby club, or small groups for a couple of families to start doing Christian life together.

Questions to consider

1 How are you doing in your own walk as a follower of Jesus?

2 Which of the five areas of the Great Commandments needs your attention at the moment? Loving God with your heart, mind, soul or strength? Or loving your neighbour as yourself?

3 How can you help people engage more with the Great Commandments and disciplines of Christian life?

4 Where do you see people of all ages encouraging each other in their journey as disciples of Jesus Christ?

5 If one church has a Lent or Advent course running, or has built up effective home groups – could they invite others from the rest of the churches in the group to join in?

Story time

A new vicar arrived in a group of churches where they expected the minister to do everything – lead, organize and take responsibility for every part of every service. He was not content to let that continue – even though it was a model well known in many churches and had been the case for many generations. He knew it was a recipe for burnout and that it led to churches full of dependent Christians who were not taking responsibility for growing in their own faith. So, very gently, he started encouraging people to have a go at new things – readings, intercessions and leading – and learning how to be disciples. The culture began to change as a result. It was slow, patient work, but the churches became healthier. The body of Christ started to function as a body and people began to grow in their faith.

One vicar asked a man in his nineties about his praying. He said: 'It takes me about two hours to get up and going in the morning. I use that time for my devotions.' It gave the vicar so much hope to know that someone in that small, ageing congregation was giving two hours a day to praying.

9

Our Faith Sharing, Part 1
Learning and practising

Always be ready to make your defence to anyone who demands from you an account of the hope that is in you. (1 Peter 3.15)

'As people's faith began to deepen, we saw them more willing to share their faith with others.' (Quote from the coalface)

Confidence

How confident are people at showing and sharing their faith across your churches? This is another area where, working across the benefice, we can encourage each other and learn together. For some of the people who come to our churches, talking about religion is something that is not considered polite, along with politics and money and other such matters. For others, they would not know where to begin in explaining why they go to church, because they have never had to. Some would assume that explaining faith and growing the church is the job of ordained and lay leaders. Others are terrified that, if they were in a conversation about faith at work, college or school, they would be asked questions they had no idea how to answer.

How can we help people to learn together about sharing their faith in a way that helps all our churches to move forward?

If we cannot help people talk with each other – in a supportive church environment – about why they treasure being followers of Jesus, they are less likely to be confident in talking with others who wonder why they still bother going to church. In a world that sees churches as, at best, extra social services – organizing toddler groups and food banks

– or, at worst, completely irrelevant to real life, we all need to be able to talk about our faith in credible, confident and kind ways.

The dreaded 'e' word

In the last two chapters we looked at the Great Commandments and the Great Commission, outlining ways to help people to grow as disciples. We reminded ourselves that our core business is making disciples – whether that is helping new believers or established saints to grow as followers of Jesus. This and the next chapter will focus on joining in with God's mission to make completely new disciples, which is the heart of the Great Commission. It is also sometimes the hardest of topics to address in our churches. Although we long for new churchgoers, we are sometimes scared – both lay people and clergy alike – of what might be required of us to give people opportunities to become disciples.

When we use the word 'evangelism' to talk about helping new people come to faith, often our faithful, current church members become even more alarmed. The stereotypes of evangelists are not always helpful – Bible bashers, street preachers loudly berating people for their sins, vast crowd events or slick salespeople who seem to have all the answers and never listen to anyone.

Perhaps we and our people hold on to these stereotypes because they let us off the hook. If we could never imagine doing evangelism like they do, then we can assume that we do not need to do it at all. Not so fast! This is a false conclusion.

If we were to ask the people in our churches to talk about those who had been instrumental in their journey of faith, a small number may mention famous evangelists or local clergy. Many more will probably talk about family members or friends who talked with them about faith, parents who taught them to pray or friends and relations who invited or took them to church.

We can therefore remind people that evangelism is most often done by ordinary people being willing to risk telling others a little about their faith, perhaps just enough to pique their interest. We may not all be gifted and effective evangelists, but we can all learn how to speak about our faith, in our own way, even if we have never done so before.

We can encourage people to look at Jesus encountering individuals in the Gospels, where it seems he had something different to say to each one. With the young fishermen, Jesus invited them to follow him to become fishers of people. With the rich young ruler, Jesus commended his understanding of the Commandments but advised him to sell all his possessions because they were a trap for him. With the Samaritan woman by the well, Jesus invited her to taste of living water, while for the paralysed man lowered through the roof, Jesus' priority was to declare his sins forgiven.

We can explore with our churches the idea of Jesus being the same yesterday, today and for ever, still treating people as individuals, with their own journeys of faith and understanding. We can encourage them to care for each of their friends, relations, colleagues and workmates as individuals who are precious to God, each with their story to tell and their own questions about the meaning of life.

The journey of faith

We all do well, too, to remember that often a journey to faith, to deciding to be a follower of Christ, can take a long time and is just that, a *journey*. There may be some who have powerful and instant conversion experiences, but for many, the journey to faith – perhaps including exploration, discussion, pondering, trying to pray, going to church, becoming part of a Christian community, reading the Bible or being part of a Christian basics course – may take many months or years. Our part is to pray and walk alongside people, making the most of chances to talk, discuss and encourage people towards commitment. While we treasure the relationships, whatever they may decide about faith, if they commit to becoming a Christian, we continue to walk alongside them, helping them to get well established in their new faith and to understand the implications of exploring the love of God in Christ.

When we encourage people to remember that most people come to faith through the friendship, witness and prayers of ordinary Christians, they begin to grow in confidence. We can then start to talk about the anxieties people have about sharing their faith. Here are some of them.

1 Fear of spoiling a friendship

Sometimes people do not want to talk about faith, or invite their friends to church services or events, because they are afraid that their friendship will be damaged in some way. Will the friend be offended? Or angry? Perhaps even abandon the relationship? These are real fears but are not an excuse for Christians to withhold from a friend the most important thing in their lives – their journey through all the challenges and joys of life with Jesus. Obviously, we all need to be tactful and respectful, but we can encourage our congregations to drop things into the conversation, mentioning, for example, why they find being part of a Christian community helpful.

2 Fear that people will not like our churches

This fear has all sorts of facets. A church member may fear bringing a friend to church on an 'off' day – when it is rather mundane and things don't flow well. They fear people being unwelcoming or awkward.

However, we can remind people to trust that God is bigger than our fears and that he can meet with visitors through any type of worship event, even one that seems dull. One recent story is of a young person who was deeply convicted of a particular sin through the general confession in a quiet, sparsely attended, early-morning BCP service, taken by a rather weary church leader.

We remind everyone that the most important thing is to pray for a friend whenever they come, to look after them during the service and keep the conversation going in the weeks to come.

3 Fear we won't know what to say

This is a big one. Christians are afraid of getting out of their depth, worrying about someone having lots of objections or asking difficult questions. We can encourage people that the main thing is to stay calm, polite and kind. If Christians get anxious or defensive, the quality of the discussion speaks louder than the content, and *that* is what will be remembered. Remind them that it is fine to go away and find out more about questions they cannot answer.

It is all about obedience

The international itinerant speaker Michael Harvey, who has done a lot of work on why people are hesitant to invite people to church, finds that these fears, plus many others, are very common among Christians in the Western world (see www.cultureofinvitation.com). However, he then challenges people to think about obedience. As disciples we are to learn to hear the nudges of the Holy Spirit and obey them – whatever the cost or outcome. Acting with love and grace, we can invite people to church-based events. They may say 'yes' or 'no'. That is not our issue. Our responsibility is to take the risk and invite them in the first place. Their response is between them and God – the God who loves them more than we ever can, whether they are a stranger or our oldest friend.

Underneath all these fears is the big one – a fear of rejection. However, as Harvey points out, we follow a Saviour who risked rejection on a world scale and sacrificed his own comfort and the glories of heaven in order to bring us back to God. Surely we too can take some risks and sacrifice our own comfort to share God's love with others? We can offer our fears of rejection to God and then find strength to keep inviting people, praying for them and being ready to give 'an account of the hope that is in us'.

We don't have to do everything

It is also important to help the people in our churches realize that, as the journey of faith takes time, they do not have to tell others everything about their faith in one go. They can pursue conversations kindly and respectfully for as long as the other person is interested, listening carefully to their stories and opinions, and aiming to help them move a little further in their journey. The Christian's job is to be available for God to use as the Holy Spirit prompts them.

One Christian met an older lady in a supermarket queue who was buying two big bunches of flowers. The Christian commented on their beauty and the lady said she was buying them for her daughter returning from hospital that day, after an operation for a serious condition. The queue was moving very fast and there was little time. The Christian did, however, ask for the woman's and her daughter's names, then said,

'I am a Christian and will pray for you both today.' The lady became a little tearful with gratitude. The Christian then kept the promise to pray during the rest of that day. She described it as a tiny encounter, but one she hoped would give a little taste of God's love to the lady buying flowers.

We are not alone

We can teach people that none of this is an individual endeavour. For a start, as we saw from looking at the framing of the Great Commission, Jesus not only declared that he has all authority in earth and heaven, but he also promised to be with us always. As we help people to embrace faith sharing, as individuals and as groups of churches, we can remind them that we are about God's business and he is with us in it.

Our church people also need to know that conversations with others about faith are a shared responsibility. Perhaps we will start gathering church people together regularly to pray for others to come to faith – to take on the Thy Kingdom Come initiative challenge to pray for five people regularly, for example (see www.thykingdomcome.global). We might start small groups who learn together how to share faith and practise doing so in a friendly environment so as to be more relaxed when opportunities arise outside of church (for more on this, see *How to Nurture a Faith-Sharing Culture*, available from https://www.cpas.org.uk/browse-everything/how-nurture-faith-sharing-culture). Perhaps we will plan a series of events across the churches – social events, enquirers' courses, special services – that are specifically aimed at newcomers and that make it easy for church people to invite their friends.

Often the stories of people coming to faith include their experience of a loving Christian community as having a significant impact on them. We – clergy and church members alike – often underestimate the treasure that we have in our churches: the seasoned, loving, committed, forgiving communities of followers of Jesus who, for all our faults and weaknesses, walk together in faith year by year, worshipping, praying and serving together.

Evangelism is a shared responsibility and a shared joy. What delight there is across our churches when we see new people come to faith and take their place in the body of Christ. We see new friendships form in the churches and new gifts released. New Christians may bring their families and friends to see the new life they have discovered. Sometimes whole families come to faith.

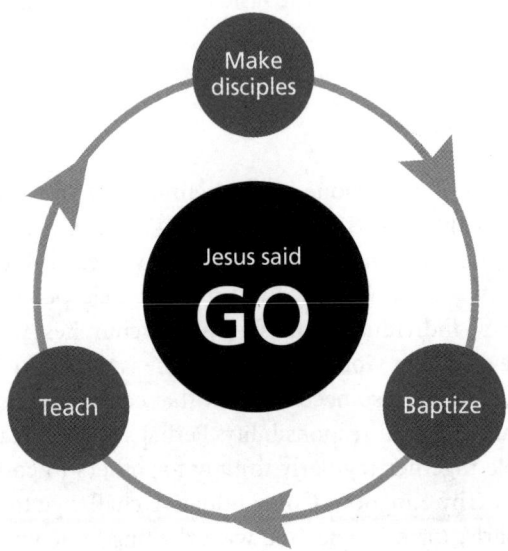

In the Great Commission, Jesus said several things, as we have seen (represented in the simple diagram above). The first of these is 'GO'.

Growing our churches is never about being in our buildings for the few short hours we are there each week and expecting people to come to us. We need to encourage our people continually that it is about our whole lives being available and open to God to use, to show and speak of his life-transforming love to others.

Baptize and teach

Helping people to come to faith is just the beginning. As we saw in the chapters on discipleship, deciding to follow Christ is the start of a journey of lifelong discipleship, learning and growth. We can work with our church people to help new Christians prepare to be baptized and, in due time, confirmed. We help them establish ways of praying that work for them. We help them to become disciples who are keen and confident to share their faith with others. Often the glorious changes that happen in people's lives as they discover the love and forgiveness of Christ have a profound impact on those around them – who then start to ask questions themselves.

We also help people discover the gifts that God has given them – so they too can be a full part of the body of Christ – when people are together in church gatherings and when they are living the rest of their lives in work and community.

The aim of all of this is that the Great Commission becomes a cycle. People come to faith, are baptized, learn and then go themselves to share that faith with others.

The scale of the challenge

In recent years there have been two rounds of research, called Talking Jesus, which have revealed a significant interest among people who are not Christians in finding out more about Christian faith (referred to in Chapter 3 here). Moreover, there was a substantial increase of interest in the years between the two rounds. Three headlines from the 2022 research are as follows:

1 A third of non-Christians, having had a conversation with a Christian (and choosing to remain a non-Christian), are open to talking more about Jesus Christ.
2 Some 36 per cent of non-Christians, having had a conversation with a Christian (and choosing to remain a non-Christian), are open to experiencing or encountering him.
3 A third of non-Christians recall being asked about what they believe when in a faith conversation with a Christian.

These headlines should give us pause – and be a cause of great encouragement. When a third of people are interested in following up a conversation with a Christian, or are hoping for an encounter with Jesus, then we have to conclude that the fields are ready for harvesting. We have often thought that it is immensely difficult to speak of our faith, to help people towards discipleship and to grow in that commitment. This research challenges us to think otherwise.

Can we mobilize our churches to grasp these opportunities, especially as the research reveals that it is particularly the younger generations who are interested in exploring Jesus and encountering him? Our challenge is to help our grandparent-aged church members share their faith with the younger people in their families, with families they may know in their communities and with younger colleagues in their places of work and leisure. When many younger people are living a long way from their own families, older friends and colleagues can be greatly valued and those relationships can open opportunities to share faith.

People are deeply hungry for authentic community. For example, there are churches with over-subscribed baby and toddler groups because young parents are desperate for good places to meet other families and share experiences and advice. In our churches, we often have hundreds of years of experience of creating loving, authentic communities. We have much to offer those outside church, of all ages.

These, therefore, are potentially great days for our churches to grow. If we can harness the possibilities of working together that come with multiple congregations, we can start to show and share the love of God more intentionally in our communities. Events or ideas don't have to be spectacular or big-budget. It is far more important that people find us friendly, caring and welcoming, whatever we do.

Send us out in the power of your Spirit

This sentence from the post-communion prayer – 'Send us out in the power of your Spirit to live and work for your praise and glory' – is one we may zip through without thought, so often have we said it. However, when we reflect on it we realize that it is a powerful and dangerous prayer to speak. It may well be worth taking some time with our congregations unpacking what this prayer is asking.

It is certainly not a prayer for those hoping that church attendance is all that is required to keep on the right side of God. It is a life-embracing prayer. It is asking that the Spirit of the Most High God should work in us in power, day by day, enabling us to live the whole of our lives in ways that bring praise and glory to God: in relating to our nearest and dearest, in our conduct in the workplace, in our leisure pursuits and in our behaviour in voluntary or community work commitments.

We are asking God to help us live lives of honesty and integrity, faith and generosity, loyalty and prayerfulness. We are asking God to help us be more and more like Jesus. And we are asking for the courage to show and share the love of God because more of the world's population, each and every one of them beloved of God, coming into the kingdom of God is what, above all, brings him praise and glory.

Practising together

Part of helping our church people become more confident about sharing their faith is ensuring they have lots of opportunities to practise: to talk about their story and to reflect with others on how God has helped them. To start with, this might seem very unfamiliar and may need to be introduced very gently.

But it can be fun. Sometimes, at a learning-community gathering, we have asked people to pair up with someone they do not know very well and to pretend that they have met in a lift. As the doors close and they start their journey to the tenth floor, one turns to the other and says: 'I've heard you are a Christian. What on earth is that all about?' That person has 60 seconds to explain their faith. Then we pretend it is the journey back down the big building and we change roles. The question this time is: 'What really important things about Christian faith do we need to pass on to younger generations?'

Once the exercise is done – often with quite a lot of laughter – we ask a few people to tell us what the *other* person in their conversation said. People are often blown away by the wise, helpful and honest things they hear. Individuals often discover that they can express things better than they ever would have guessed.

Another exercise you can do, in small groups, is to discuss and reflect on real-life opportunities you have all had to share faith, both the ones that have gone well and those that have seemed really difficult. All are worth discussing and learning from. You can also think together about possible responses to common objections to faith.

The point of all these exercises is that the more we practise, the readier we become to talk with those who would not call themselves Christians, and the easier we find it.

The readier we are to talk, and to listen carefully to other people's stories of what they believe about the meaning of life, the more likely we are to have the extraordinary joy of seeing new people come to faith across our churches.

Enquirers' courses

In the past, many people learned the basic stories and beliefs of the Christian faith in different settings, through Sunday school, weekday schools, catechism, baptism and confirmation classes or at home. The festivals of the Christian year were community-wide occasions. Clergy could assume that there was a base level of understanding. These days, increasing numbers of people, especially in younger generations, know nothing of Christian faith or only see the caricatures of Christians and clergy that the media portray.

This may be a reason why enquirers' courses have proved so helpful in recent decades. They can have various effects on different people. They may:

1 Take people from knowing very little to understanding what being a Christian entails, in terms of belief and belonging to a Christian community.
2 Create a safe space for people to ask the big questions of life and have the chance to explore their own life journey. For many people, there are few opportunities to do that in the course of normal life.
3 Provide a refresher course for the people in our churches, or even help them understand things they have never addressed before. One lady, after coming to an enquirers' session about Jesus, said in wonder afterwards, 'Oh, so Jesus was *God* ...' She had been in church circles all her life, and somehow this had never fallen into place for her until this session.
4 Finally, they may provide great opportunities for the people in our churches, again in a safe environment, to witness to their own faith to others who are not yet Christians, as they discuss questions together.

Questions to consider

1 Take some time to think about the churches and congregations across your group. How well are they doing at equipping their members to show and share their faith in the rest of their lives? What good things are happening that you can share around the churches to encourage everyone?

2 Who might be willing to work in a cross-benefice evangelism team?

3 What social occasions for newcomers could be created? What enquirers' events could be put on for adults, for young people or for families?

Story time

One group of churches started serving tea and toast in the church building that the teenagers passed on their way home from school (with all appropriate safeguarding measures in place). It was a simple idea and, after a very slow start, became hugely popular. Friendships were formed and questions were asked. Small steps to enable these young people to explore the Christian faith were taken.

Some church toddler groups that have no Christian content in their gathering time are showing and sharing their faith more explicitly with the attending families. They do not change anything about the session – people still get what they have signed up for. However, they do offer an extra 10 or 15 minutes on the end for those who choose to stay. In that time, they tell a simple Bible story to both children and adults, sing some Christian children's songs and invite children and adults to suggest items for prayer that they then pray about in a straightforward way.

One saint in his eighties, from a village church, was desperate to share his faith. He and a few others planned a morning event at the local pub, with hot drinks and bacon rolls for all. A story-teller was invited to come and talk about people's journeys to faith, both contemporary and from the Scriptures. They printed beautiful hand-designed invitations and spent weeks giving them to anyone and everyone in the village and neighbouring villages in the MPB. The morning came and around 45 adults came to hear stories of Jesus, to feast on the food and to ask questions about Christian faith. The man afterwards wondered why church services were so off-putting to newcomers compared to this relaxed sharing of hospitality, time, input, discussion and conversation.

During lockdown, one church primary school encouraged teachers and local church leaders to record content for school assemblies for those children who had to be in school and the vast majority who were at home. Those assemblies were made available through the school website. They discovered that whole families were engaging with the assemblies together at home, finding them helpful. Even now, with the school open as normal, they are keen to keep school assemblies available online.

10

Our Faith Sharing, Part 2

Events and involvement

Peter replied, 'Repent and be baptised, every one of you, in the name of Jesus Christ for the forgiveness of your sins. And you will receive the gift of the Holy Spirit.' (Acts 2.38 NIV)

'Our summer lunch event gathered people from the churches and local communities across the benefice.' (Quote from the coalface)

Going and coming

In the last chapter we talked about how Jesus instructs us to GO to make disciples of all nations. In this chapter we look at ways of witnessing to our faith beyond our gathering in church buildings: through different spaces and through different mission interests. Then we consider how well we welcome people to our churches and look at the different types of new and inspiring church initiatives that are happening around the country.

Places – onsite, online, outside

The pandemic and accompanying lockdowns pushed many of our churches to GO into new spaces with the gospel. Many churches have started, and continue to occupy, online space, having never done so before, often with unexpected success. Churches and leaders that might never have expected to go digital have discovered that they are taking the gospel to the nations almost unintentionally, as visitors from around the world join them for their online services and events.

Many churches also had to GO outside their buildings. With extraordinary creativity, churches have hosted pilgrimages, churchyard trails, treasure hunts, forest churches, services and so on, in the great outdoors.

Was God, in the midst of all that was so hard in the pandemic, opening up new spaces for us to show and share our faith?

One church was delighted when a large congregation of people stayed for the whole of a Remembrance service, because it was all outside, when in previous years, most of them would have peeled off once the short act of remembrance was over at the war memorial, and the usual congregation headed off into the building.

Research is also clear that, where churches are continuing to give people the chance to join online, they are doing better in terms of overall numbers than those that have abandoned online options (Dr Bev Botting, Ven Bob Jackson, 'Easter Church Attendance Report 2022', available from CPAS).

Of course, there are significant logistical and practical challenges here, in terms of the people needed to enable both onsite and online services and events, as well as how to do things outside our buildings. Here, once again, churches in an MPB are at an advantage because perhaps only one service across the whole benefice needs to be online in order for people to join, whether they are housebound, wanting to take a look at church before coming across the threshold, shielding or caring for sick relatives. Perhaps one MPB church could hold an outdoor event as an extra, to which the other churches, and communities they represent, are invited.

The Five Marks of Mission

For around 40 years, The Five Marks of Mission have inspired Anglican churches around the world in their work of witness and mission. Originally developed by the Anglican Consultative Council in 1984, they have been adopted by Anglican churches around the world. They are:

1 To proclaim the good news of the kingdom.
2 To teach, baptize and nurture new believers.

3 To respond to human need by loving service.

4 To seek to transform unjust structures of society, to challenge violence of every kind and to pursue peace and reconciliation.

5 To strive to safeguard the integrity of creation and sustain and renew the life of the earth.

These essential characteristics of mission in its widest sense help us to think through what we are doing.

These Marks set people free to do the things that God is calling them to do. Different people have God-given passions for different things. In a world where the climate crisis is climbing higher and higher up the agenda, the fifth one might be a call to action for many people. However, across an MPB, all these Marks are relevant to all our churches, even if the best way to achieve successful action might be by creating focus groups across the group of churches.

It is also true that the first Mark is sometimes the one we struggle with most. For all the reasons we looked at in the last chapter, often the hardest thing of all is to talk about our faith with others, offer to say a prayer with someone in need or invite people we know to one of our churches. People in many churches find it easier to do things like:

- welcome people to the baptism of a family member
- help people grow in faith
- serve our communities with food banks or baby groups
- join campaigning organizations or charities for justice or ecology

... than to actually talk about their own faith.

Some people consider the first Mark of Mission as an umbrella statement of what all mission is about, because it is based on Jesus' own summary of his mission (Matthew 4.17, Mark 1.14–15, Luke 4.18–19, Luke 7.22; John 3.14–17).

Our unique offering to a world facing multiple crises is the good news of Jesus. So if the first Mark of Mission is an umbrella for all the others, whichever of the others people in our churches concentrate on, the key is that they are doing it in a way that shows and shares their faith in Jesus. Even when we are working on these issues in partnership with other – perhaps secular – organizations, we are still called to demonstrate the love of Christ.

Welcoming

It is no good our people showing and sharing faith in all they do if our churches are not places of warm and kind welcome. In Chapter 4 we talked about doing great hospitality across our churches. We considered it vital that we rediscover the art of great Christian hospitality – generous, open-hearted, creative and genuinely welcoming. This spills over into our consideration of evangelism and witness. If the homes of our church members across our communities become increasingly places of welcome (where culturally appropriate), and if our churches embrace the need to be joyfully and sensitively welcoming of all, then more people will be attracted to faith.

Consider the following scenarios.

Scenario 1

Someone comes timidly to the door of one of our churches for the first time. The day is cold and the door is closed to keep in the warmth. The newcomer has to work out how to open the ancient door with its giant, noisy latch. Inside, someone greets them and hands them several books. The newcomer finds a seat, having come in good time. Then someone comes and asks them to move because that is 'their seat'. Embarrassed, the newcomer moves, a little further to the front. By the time the service starts, no one has sat in front of them or even near them. This means they cannot see what other people are doing during the service and so they find it hard to know how to negotiate the books they have and when to sit or stand.

At the time for communion – a whole new experience for the newcomer – someone kindly comes and invites them to go forward. But because they are at the front, they have no idea what that might mean and so stay firmly seated while watching others.

At the end of the service, they are invited to have a cuppa at the back, which is very welcome, but then no one really speaks to them and they are left to stand or sit alone while animated conversations between old friends go on around them. They leave as soon as possible and vow not to return.

Scenario 2

Someone new approaches one of our churches for the first time. On the old thick door is a welcome notice that explains that the door is kept closed for warmth, but that they are very welcome. Perhaps there is even a church member waiting outside to greet people and let them in – because that door handle is something of a problem. Inside, they are warmly greeted and given some books. Someone asks if they know their way around the books and, upon hearing that they don't, explains a few things to the newcomer. They then take them to sit with someone in the congregation, not too near the front, who can be relied on to be friendly and to explain to them what is happening and where to find things, without being too intrusive.

At the time for communion, the person sitting with the newcomer explains what is going on and invites them to come to the front with them for communion or a blessing, showing them what to do. After the service, the friendly person invites the newcomer to coffee, taking care to introduce them to a few people and keeping an eye out for when the newcomer might be left stranded with no one to talk to. The newcomer is encouraged to fill in a contact card, but without pressure. They leave feeling warmed and welcomed. When an email arrives inviting them back the next week, and to a social event at someone's house the week after that, they consider it carefully and with real interest.

Mystery worshipper

Some MPBs have sent a 'mystery worshipper' to the other churches in the group, preferably someone unknown to the other churches. Their role is to look carefully at all the things that would proclaim welcome, or otherwise, to newcomers. Some of the things they might consider are:

- Is there any online information about that church – as part of a benefice site or on social media? Is the information welcoming, accurate and up to date? Has old information been taken down? Is it easy to find the information about services?
- Are the notice boards up to date and interesting? Are there photos of key office holders in the church?

- Are there things that children would notice as they come into the building that tell them they are welcome? Perhaps a welcome sign at child height, a play corner, bags of quiet toys to play with during the service; or artwork done by children displayed prominently and kept fresh?
- Are newcomers welcomed specifically, at every service?
- Are clear explanations given during the service as to what to do? Do any service books explain why we say and do the different things that happen?
- If there are refreshments before or after the service, are the drinks and eats of good quality? Are those who serve friendly and willing?
- Are newcomers introduced to others who will take an interest in them?
- Are there welcome cards or other ways for people to give their contact details if they would like to do so? Does someone then follow those up?

Our commitment to welcoming newcomers, week after week, year after year, really matters. And sometimes we have to look in detail at every part of our welcome to see whether it is really working, or how we could do it better. Often, it is when newcomers are befriended by people like them – families by other families, newly retireds by others newly retired, teenagers by teenagers and so on – that they start to feel they really belong.

And how about our welcome to people online? If we have the resources, then having someone to interact with online attenders during a service can make them feel both welcome and involved. This might well become increasingly important in the years to come.

Keeping

We also need to pay attention to keeping people in our churches. It is all too easy for people gradually to stop coming, without anyone really noticing. It is all too easy for people to start questioning their faith in very deep ways and not have anyone to talk with, or for people to get out of the habit of coming to church, onsite or online, and nobody seeming to care. Especially in a climate where, for many people, regular church attendance means once or twice a month, rather than weekly, looking out for every individual is so important.

People stay in churches where they are:

- Loved and cared for.
- Growing in faith.
- Feel safe.
- Equipped to live as disciples and witnesses in every part of their lives.
- And, crucially, aware there is a sense of purpose and direction.

Would people find these ingredients across our churches? This list can make overall leaders panic, wondering how we can possibly provide all those things across multiple churches, as well as keep up with all the admin, safeguarding, rotas, occasional offices, relationship issues and the crises that are part and parcel of church leadership. This is why we looked earlier in the book at the need to find and grow new leaders. They make it possible, together across the MPBs, to begin to cover all these bases and maximize the strengths of each church community.

New initiatives

In the past few decades, one of the most fruitful ways of bringing the gospel to people has been through starting whole new church communities. Reviewing with our churches what has been happening in this area might well start people dreaming of new possibilities. For example:

1 Church plants

The more familiar of these new churches have been church plants. These are, as most people know, where a group of people from one church move into a new area where there is no church already, or where there is a church that needs revitalising, and together they plant a new Christian community. The main characteristic of church plants is that they take the DNA of the planting church with them. The new church will share many of the practices, theological understandings and styles of the church they came from. They start with worship with the intention of blessing the community they are planted in, caring for it and drawing people into Christian faith. They are a vital part of the growth of the Church across the nation. In the past they may well have been called mission churches or daughter churches. They provide great opportunities for people to do mission and evangelism together and they bring new life in all sorts of places, including inner cities, difficult estates and rural areas.

2 Resource churches

Some of the newest of these church plants have been designated 'resource churches' and have been given financial help to get them started. The hope for these is that they will become vibrant Christian communities that, in time, will be able to extend help to other churches around them. They too are a vital part of our work to grow the Church across the nation.

3 Fresh expressions of church

In addition, since the Mission-shaped Church report of 2004, people have been starting fresh expressions of church. The impetus for these comes from the understanding that for many, the culture of our inherited churches is never going to be helpful to them in exploring faith. For those of us who have grown up going to church, that is not always easy to understand, because it all seems normal to us.

For those planting fresh expressions of church, however, they are taking the GO part of Jesus' Great Commission very seriously indeed. Their aim is to get to know a particular group of people in the community – perhaps families, disaffected young people, people working in a specific industry or homeless people – by serving them in some way. Perhaps they start a food bank, toddler group, café, social event or some other regular event that creates community. As they get to know people, their aim is to start faith conversations with them and eventually to create a worship event that is culturally appropriate to that group of people. They place a high value on making and growing new disciples. Intriguingly, while such a fresh expression of church may start with a particular group of people, often others – family members, friends, people of different ages – are drawn to it as well by the vitality and community they see there. Perhaps the versions most familiar to us are café churches, Messy churches and forest churches.

Such fresh expressions of church have seen large numbers of people drawn into Christian faith and church life. Some of those new Christians may well end up moving on to the inherited or traditional churches in their location. For others, the new church will always be their home. Obviously, as the new fresh expression adds more of the practices of being church, even if they are expressed in a way that is culturally different, they become established churches in their own right. These fresh expressions of church are vital to the growth of the Church across the UK and beyond.

Growing to maturity

The real sign of maturity of new churches – whether church plants or fresh expressions – is when they are ready to send out a group to start another new church community.

It is easy to criticize, judge or be resentful of these new initiatives, but we would do well to refrain from that and be supportive. It may well be that these new churches are just as important to God for the growth of his kingdom as the faithful, prayerful, inherited churches who often provide people and finance for the new approaches as well as for their own needs.

It is so encouraging to see the creativity, energy, commitment, dogged persistence and resilience that is to be found in followers of Jesus when churches across MPBs work together across traditional *and* new types of church.

Congregations in healthy MPBs have the potential to create innovations such as breakfast churches, Messy churches, pizza churches for teenagers and so on. They will find that working together gives them strengths, resources and underpinning prayer that they would never have on their own.

Questions to consider

1 Put aside some time, preferably with others, to look at each of the Five Marks of Mission. Write down what you are doing to fulfil each one of them across your churches. How could you do all of them in a way that proclaims the good news?

2 How welcoming are your churches? Really? Are newcomers cared for and looked after until they feel they genuinely belong and have friends of their own?

3 How do your churches keep in contact with their members? Do you have home groups or prayer groups? How do you make sure people don't slip away unnoticed?

4 As you assess your churches, where do you see new gifts being discovered and used?

5 What new initiatives are happening across your churches? Are people – young Christians and more established ones – dreaming of possibilities and being supported to make them happen?

Story time

Messy churches have been remarkably successful, not just in the UK, but around the world. Groups of tiny rural churches have often found that, by working together, they can start and grow a Messy church in a location where most of the families live. The challenge is always to keep the focus on helping people come to faith and growing new disciples, rather than just putting on great events for families.

Some churches discovered more people who were willing to step up and take part in services during the months we were all online. Singers, musicians, intercessors, readers, those giving testimonies – many new people recorded themselves for online services or took part in Zoom events. These things grow confidence in speaking up about faith, both inside and outside the churches. In a world where the online space is increasingly important, we can build on this momentum.

11

Our Future, Part 1

Assessing and prioritizing

Do all things without murmuring and arguing, so that you may be blameless and innocent, children of God without blemish in the midst of a crooked and perverse generation, in which you shine like stars in the world. (Philippians 2.14–15)

'Just as in marriage preparation, when we help a couple to think through their expectations, communication and past baggage, so it is important to help an MPB think through what change will look like, what compromises need to be made and what benefits will result.' (Quote from the coalface)

Where have we got to?

If you have been taking time to muse on the questions at the end of each chapter, or if you have been using this book alongside the downloadable course, then we have been on a significant journey together. You may well have started making some small changes that are beginning to affect the culture across the churches in which you lead.

Perhaps you have been encouraging people to pray – publicly and privately – for the life and witness of your churches, and seen some answers to those prayers, using the *Thrive Prayer Guide* as inspiration.

Perhaps you have explored together the journey of your churches – how you came together, what the high points and challenges have been along the way and the next steps that God might be calling you to take.

Perhaps you have started praying for, looking for and training up new leaders, including some children and young people.

Perhaps you have considered whether those in your churches are, or are not, growing in their own walk as disciples of Christ and discovered ways to help them along the journey.

Perhaps you have worked together on the challenges of mission and evangelism – seeing your churches increase in confidence in showing and sharing their faith. This may have resulted in some cross-church explorers' courses or the starting of a fresh expression of church.

A new star

Now we start to think about the future. In this chapter we will use the star diagram we talked about in Chapter 1 to review where we have got to, think about possible shorter-term plans for the future and prioritize what is important. In the next chapter we will think more about long-term vision for our churches.

If you have made some small steps of progress, then this is the time to review the star you filled in at the start of the book. It is time to reflect again on how the churches you lead and oversee are doing in the first five of the six different areas we have studied. You may want to add to the first star or fill out a new one. The hope and prayer is that you will see that there has been real progress.

If, along with reading this book, you have been doing the Thrive course as well with a cross-MPB team, then do take your time over this review. And enjoy the process. This is not intended as a deadly serious thing to do. Have fun filling in the new star with colours, words and diagrams to show the progress you have made.

What next?

It is also possible that you have got this far in the book and pondered things carefully, but have yet to take any action.

Whether you have started work or want to survey the scene before committing to action, you may well be full of questions. What is the wider picture? Do we need a bigger vision for the churches than just working on these different areas? How do we get started and how do we maintain momentum?

Here are three possible short-term ways forward. You could choose one or combine them in some way.

1 Annual star review

You could decide to adopt the star as an annual plan for the next few years, working your way around the six areas each year or every two years, and taking action to introduce improvements so that each year your new star becomes more complete, with your churches working, growing and doing mission more effectively. It is a simple and clear way forward.

The leadership enablers' team at CPAS came across an inspiring example of this. Once a year the team visits a business or organization in order to learn from its leadership style. One year we were privileged to visit a distribution warehouse of a major online sales company. It was a fascinating visit and we came away with much to think about, both helpful and critical. However, one thing stood out and has remained with me very clearly.

As a sales company, Christmas was their most important time of the year. So they dedicated significant energy, time and resources to making it as successful as possible. What struck me was that the review of the success, or otherwise, of their Christmas efforts began in a disciplined way at the beginning of each new year. They analysed the metrics and procedures rigorously and started planning for the following Christmas right then.

I came away wondering what it would be like for groups of churches to have planning teams for Christmas – and other big events – who were always reaching for ways to engage more effectively with those who come to them for the kingdom of God: always willing to review and to make helpful changes; investing resources into creative and more effective activities and approaches rather than repeating the previous ones. There are, of course, MPBs that already do this, but it would be a challenge to others. In times when people consider the church as a nice idea or a helpful social service but largely irrelevant spiritually, let us make the absolute most of the big occasions through the year when larger numbers of people from the community may join us – whether online, onsite or outside. How can these events increasingly help people discover some of the riches of Christ in their own lives?

That is just one example but it shows the value of choosing to review your star annually or biennially. You might want to keep your collection of stars over several years to track the encouraging progress.

2 Pick up specific areas

It may well be that as you have worked through the five of the six areas we have looked at so far, there are one or two that seemed so lacking that you consider the best way forward is to concentrate your energies there for the next year or two. If, for example, you realized that the congregations in your churches have not grasped the need to be disciples and to grow in their faith, that could be your priority for the near future. You don't ignore the other areas but you focus on that one.

Or again, perhaps you think that the thing you need most of all is more leaders. So that becomes your priority. You start to look for people willing to take small responsibilities and help them to grow in confidence and faith, always looking for ways they could develop. Perhaps you launch a Christian leadership course, such as Growing Leaders, downloadable from the CPAS website. Or you look outside your current congregations for young parents, school governors or others who might be interested in helping out at church and exploring faith at the same time. Whatever you do, this becomes your top priority for prayer and action.

Once those specific areas are in a better state, you might then adopt option 1 above.

3 Concentrate on one bigger project

This third option will work best when all parts of your star are looking reasonably healthy. You are confident that, across your churches, each of these areas is part of their ongoing life. In this state you decide to work together on your vision for the future. We will look at creating a vision statement in the next chapter. Here the pertinent question is: 'Is there something particular God is calling you to do together across your churches?'

For example, one group of churches in a wealthy area wanted to support some sort of overseas development project. They researched carefully to find one that genuinely established local ownership and growth of the initiatives, then funded them for several years. Many good things came out of this. Thousands of pounds were raised in the process. Churches worked together more than before and they came to understand the lives of the people in that country more fully. Many children in the country went through secondary education who would otherwise not have been able to afford it; income-generating schemes were established and work skills training given. In addition, some UK church members – teenagers and adults – visited the projects and found themselves overwhelmed by the hospitality offered by the very poorest people. The people themselves were, in turn, deeply encouraged that others from across the world would visit them and support their projects.

Many groups of churches could tell such stories. For this group it was one outworking of their vision statement. For another group it might be the setting up of a food bank. Or creating a team of listeners to volunteer in a local school to spend time with children who need them. The opportunities are limitless.

What bigger project might God be calling your churches to undertake?

Tackling a topic together

Whichever option or combination of options your group chooses, it is best to appoint a cross-benefice action team to take matters forward. Do make use of the 'explore, plan, act, review' approach too (as suggested in the Introduction; it is also integral to the Thrive course). With a committed MPB action team, it is more than possible over the course of two full years to:

1 Consider and explore a topic of church life together.
2 Decide on some actions to work on that topic over the next few months and make a plan.
3 Pray for and work on that plan across the churches for those months.
4 Review the plan at the end of the time and, while still keeping that plan moving forward, move on to the next topic.

Dealing with conflict

Your vision and planning group will need resilience to respond well, with kindness and persistence, when opposition arises to changes they start to initiate. Even small changes can meet with huge resistance.

For example, a small group from across a benefice gets excited by their discussions, their prayers and their plans about a specific topic. They then start to talk to their churches and try to implement their plans, only to come up against a brick wall. For all sorts of reasons, people are not open to even talking about changes, which can be very disheartening. While it is normal for some people to find change hard to handle, if the small group listens well and aims to help people see the advantages of new ways, if they can regroup, pray and persist for long enough, they can come through the period of opposition and start to see changes, such as new people coming, new initiatives happening, better welcoming and so on.

When the group faces opposition there are various possible responses. Here are some of them.

Frequently, many conversations with individuals are needed to get things moving. It is often worth talking specifically with the people who, while not recognized leaders in the church, yet hold influence over people's opinions. If you can get them on board it helps move the churches forward. In having such conversations we have to tackle the resistance many of us have to facing difficult issues with others. We need to remember that the issues will not conveniently go away if we ignore them. Indeed, they may well prove harder to deal with further down the line than if we had addressed them early on. The challenge, as always, is to remain calm ourselves and to communicate well – and to remember that good relationships matter profoundly in the kingdom of God.

It may be that the issues are best talked through in small groups or in PCCs or a Group Council. The material about creating great teams is relevant here (see Chapter 6). In talking about difficult issues, the way that they are introduced and framed is really important in creating a trusting atmosphere where people can have their say.

Alternatively, wider meetings across the benefice – perhaps in a pub with a meal – for all those interested in the proposals give everyone the chance to air their opinions. Thorough advance planning about content, presentation and possible question-and-answer sessions is vital if such an event is to go well.

It would be easy to abandon the dreams at the point when conflict arises. However, if the group can continue to pray and plan, if they can carry on taking small, determined steps of progress, if they can keep the conversations with individuals, groups and PCCs open and friendly, eventually most people will come on board. It will certainly help if everyone is asked to pray for the future of the churches in the group, making use of the *Thrive Prayer Guide*. It is also helpful to continue to speak of the plans as having come from the action team working together. That way, no one individual is likely to be picked on. Keep going; don't give up.

Jesus knows

So many of the Gospel records are of Jesus having difficult or contentious conversations with individuals or groups of people. Whether it was his close disciples who did not understand his stories or decisions, or religious leaders trying to trip him up, Jesus was faced again and again with hostile comments and questions. He addressed these in different ways – sometimes with strong challenge, sometimes with a prophetic story or action, sometimes with gentle explanation. Of course, ultimately, for Jesus the conflict led to the cross. Then he turned everything on its head in his resurrection from the dead and ascension into heaven. He proved what he had said: 'In this world you will have trouble. But take heart! I have overcome the world' (John 16.33 NIV).

Like us, Jesus was faced with those who wanted everything to stay the same, those who were radical and wanted to change everything drastically, and everyone in between. Sometimes, like him, we need to set our faces (Luke 9.51) in the direction we believe that God is calling us to follow and keep going.

The joyful truth for us is that, as we saw in Chapter 7, Jesus' promise to be with us always keeps us in a strong place, whatever the cost of following his call. He completely understands what we are going through.

Communications

Crucial to all of this is the constant issue of great communication. It's hard enough in one church or in one church with more than one distinct congregation. It's an enormous challenge over a number of churches and new initiatives spread across a wide geographical area in an MPB. When you add in the number of different platforms that currently exist for conveying information, it is essential to keep addressing the effectiveness of all of them.

That is why, on the action-planning sheets for our Thrive collection of resources, there is always one section to fill in about how the group is going to convey its plans to all the churches and congregations, all the groups and, where relevant, local communities too. Communication is something we need to give attention to every time we make a plan. Part of the role of a leader is to communicate the vision and attendant plans to everyone in multiple ways, on multiple occasions, far more times than we could ever believe necessary.

So it's worth taking time to review how well your communication of all types are working at the moment. You might want to:

- Review your internet presence – the effectiveness of your websites to give newcomers and current church members the information and routes for help they might need. Is the content relevant and expressed in language that everyone can understand, not just insiders?
- Look at your social media use – is it open and friendly? Does it help people understand about the faith and work of the churches? (For example, does anyone outside of church congregations keep track of what Sunday of the month it is? Wouldn't lists of dates be easier?)
- Consider how easy it is for people to contact the churches, by email, phone and website message. Who will respond to people making enquiries and how quickly?
- What about your paper communications? Are your notice sheets or magazines communicating in easily accessible ways?
- Remember your notice boards. Are they up to date, attractive, interesting and not overwhelmed with information? Is it easy for people to find out what they need to know?

- Ask who of your leaders is the best communicator in different forms of media, including by personal and public presentation – how can you make the most of their gifts in conveying new visions and plans?
- Check that the messaging across all these different platforms and methods of communication is consistent. A typo or late posting of information can cause huge confusion.
- Know who is responsible for ensuring that you are adhering to both General Data Protection Regulation (GDPR) and safeguarding laws in your handling of data and social-media usage.
- Ask for a visit from a mystery worshipper to see what you have missed!

Questions to consider

1 As you review where you have got to across your churches so far, what good stories do you have to tell?

2 Looking at your newly filled-in star, what strikes you?

3 What is your instinct about the three possible ways forward outlined in this chapter?

4 Will you use the explore, plan, act, review cycle as you go forward (the Thrive course has more on this)? Have you added in any other stages and how have they helped? How will you use the cycle as you go forward?

5 What wisdom can you contribute to a group discussion on the subject of conflict? When have you seen it handled well and what have you learned from that? Likewise, what have you learned from seeing conflict handled badly?

6 Which Gospel stories of Jesus dealing with hostility and conflict inspire you? Why is that?

7 Regarding questions around good communications, which issues are the most pressing ones? What could you do about them?

8 How can you encourage and inspire the people across your churches to take responsibility for exploring, planning, acting and reviewing courageously and well?

9 How can you encourage everyone to be attentive to how God might be prompting, and ready to follow his leading?

Story time

Some churches around the country, faced with tiny elderly congregations and possible closure of their buildings, have opted to become 'festival churches'. They are consulting carefully with their local communities, the other churches in the benefice and with the diocese. Rather than exhausting dwindling energies by trying to continue weekly services, they are concentrating their efforts on well-run services just at the big festival occasions of the year. They are exploring partnerships too, enabling sharing of their buildings, so that more people from the communities are becoming involved in care for the buildings, and attending the big events and services. These initiatives are releasing new vitality and creativity. Like a car being taken down a gear in order to go up a hill, who knows what God might do in the future as a result?

The action team for another MPB group of churches reviewed where they had got to at the end of a learning-community gathering. They concluded that they had some things from their various action plans that they still wanted to put into practice, but they were keen also to look at their longer-term future. They decided to create an overall vision statement for the whole benefice, and then work out how the statement best applied to each of the churches and fresh expressions.

12

Our Future, Part 2

Working on vision

'And afterwards, I will pour out my Spirit on all people. Your sons and daughters will prophesy, your old men will dream dreams, your young men will see visions.' (Joel 2.28 NIV)

'The vision for the churches in our benefice is to be Jesus-centred, prayer-based, mission-focused and relationships-orientated.' (Quote from the coalface)

Do we need a vision?

So far in this book we have looked at praying, thinking and planning for ways we can start to enhance our life and work in a variety of areas. Now we want to think more widely and over the longer term.

From the last few years we know, of course, that our dreams and visions can, in a moment, be turned on their heads by world events, but that is no excuse not to have them in the first place. We can change the direction of our churches very quickly in response to huge upheaval – as we all discovered when we had to go online with our services and imagine new ways to do our pastoral care, community service, our growing of disciples and our evangelism. It is very demanding but it can be done. However, it is easier if the churches have a vision for growth already rather than going from a standing start, just as it is easier to turn the wheel of a moving vehicle to set a new direction than it is a stationary one. We might be wary of working on a vision not because of changing world events, but because of changes in the diocese. What if our benefice has to absorb more churches or be reshaped more radically?

What if there are major changes of stipendiary ordained leaders or lay leaders?

All of these are valid concerns but we should not allow them to paralyse us. Our faithful God calls us to be bold and visionary and to take risks in his name to grow his kingdom. Working on a vision is time well spent.

What is your vision?

What is your vision for your group of churches? What would be your best hope for them? How would you best like them to be working – sharing their resources and strengths, encouraging each other, yet each thriving in all that God has called them to be?

We often find the idea of vision confusing. Is it a mission state-ment? Or a set of values? Is it an impossible dream? Or something so wide-ranging that we wonder how it can ever be put into practice?

For our purposes here, we will use this definition of vision: 'A picture or description of what we would like to see happening in three to five years from now.' As you read that, what springs to mind as potential answers to that question? In this chapter we will explore ways of helping MPBs create their own vision. First, however, we need to look at some of the issues around vision.

Past experiences

What experience have you had of people working with a vision? Perhaps in a business setting, a voluntary organization or in a church or group of churches?

In some cases the careful creation of a vision inspires great energy and creativity and gives everyone focus to pursue a series of activities to bring the vision to reality. In other cases the vision may be worked on with great enthusiasm but then is allowed to fall by the wayside as the realities of day-to-day work take over.

Yet again, the vision may provide challenging direction and focus for some years, but then no thought is given to what might be the next vision and things start to stagnate.

It is not so simple, then, to create, work with and bring to completion a vision and then work on what comes next.

However, you might also have experience of a church or group of churches without any sense of clear direction. What was that like? Was there growth or difficulty? It is worth talking about these experiences with the group tasked with defining vision to see how people's past experiences affect the way they view the concept of vision. Are they hope-filled or, rather, weary or even cynical? Getting these feelings and thoughts out in the open and talking about them clears the air for constructive work on vision.

Multiple visions

For MPBs it can get extraordinarily complicated when we start working on a three-year vision, because there are potentially many layers of church initiative to bear in mind. Consider the following factors.

There is a clear vision statement for the whole Church of England for the 2020s. It was created after much consultation, prayer and thought. It is both bold and challenging and we would be wise to take it into account as we work on our own vision for our MPB. The vision is stated thus: 'A Church for the whole nation which is Jesus Christ-centred, and shaped by the Five Marks of Mission. A church that is simpler, humbler, bolder.'

This vision is then unpacked with three priorities:

1 To become a church of missionary disciples.
2 To be a church where mixed ecology is the norm.
3 To be a church that is younger and more diverse.
    (To see more on this, go to: https://www.churchofengland.org/about/vision-and-strategy.)

You may decide to adopt this vision as it is for your own churches, or adapt it to your circumstances.

Your diocese probably has a vision statement or a set of priorities for the next few years. Again, it will have been created with consultation, prayer and thought. For some dioceses, their vision statement will shape almost everything they do. As they create their own vision or mission action plan, your churches would do well to see how they can contribute to the diocesan dream. Again, you may decide to adopt the diocesan vision as it is for your churches, or adapt or add to it.

As if these were not enough, your deanery or mission area might also have its own vision. It may be more of a mission action plan, with commitments about stipendiary clergy numbers, finances and buildings. It may also have sections on working together across the deanery and hopes and dreams for the future. Again, if there is an actual vision statement here, you may decide to adopt it, adapt it or add to it.

These three layers of vision statements can seem rather overwhelming for the group of people trying to create vision across an MPB. How can your churches take their place in the overall vision for the Church of England? In the diocese? In the deanery or mission area? These are all good questions to ask, but it can get even more complicated. Oh yes.

Whole-MPB vs individual-church visions

When we get to the level of the MPB, we can find that even here, one vision does not fit all. Even though one of the great strengths of churches being grouped together is that none of them has to do everything, this can create further complications. It is not realistic for small country churches, nor struggling urban or suburban ones, to try to cater for every need, every age group, and think about doing new things. In creating a vision for your churches, then, it might well be about an overarching MPB vision, plus individual ones for each church. In assessing the gifts and callings of the different churches, you might discover initiatives or ministries that work best in just one church or a couple of churches working together. Other things might work best across the whole benefice.

For example, in one group the churches together decided on their overall vision statement. Then each church explored its own charism, its own calling, and focused its vision mainly on one or two things. One village with a church school concentrated on work with children. Another became a place for healing prayer and pilgrimage. Another grew its own worship band, which collected people from across the benefice and played for events in its own church and for group services.

Another had enough people for a formal choir, which also sang for group occasions.

In another group the churches identified things that worked best at a whole-benefice level. Marriage preparation and youth work were only viable when the churches all contributed people and resources.

As we think about vision, therefore, there is much to consider. However, there is also much to give thanks for in the work already done in other areas of the Church of England's life. These visions worked out elsewhere might inspire great starting points, or one of them could easily become our own vision statement.

This is group work

It is easy for people to believe in the heroic leader – the one who rides into town with a clear vision of what the future should look like and effortlessly draws people in to work for it and achieve even more than they set out to do. It is not a very Christian way of doing things but it is a legend that persists even in church circles. The reality is that all leaders need to work with others to create and realize a vision. Even the most impressive (or terrifying) of heroic leaders in world history would have been nothing without people working with them and alongside them – willingly or not.

In the New Testament, we see St Paul starting churches in different places on his travels and appointing groups of people as elders to lead them. Responsibility for rooting and growing these churches was something to share (Acts 20.17–38).

In a complex world, with all the other vision statements we have already mentioned, working out the vision that God is calling you to pursue in your patch needs to be a group endeavour. In order to glean as much wisdom as possible, consult widely across your churches, asking people of all ages what they think God is saying. Then a small group representing the whole benefice needs to look through all the material from elsewhere, sift through the local responses, pray and craft and refine until the vision is clear. That small group or team may already be established if you have been working on the questions in this book or doing the Thrive course.

The value of wide consultation can hardly be overstated. If you have consulted well – if you have let people know what is happening and given them the opportunity to have their say – you are likely to get them buying in to the vision across the MPB.

Dreaming of possibilities

If you have been doing the group action plans from the downloadable Thrive course, or have been working through this book with others and making changes across your churches in response to what you have read, then you have a group of people who have started to get used to working together. If they have seen some good progress on the subjects we have studied together, then your group will be more confident in dreaming and planning for a longer-term vision.

Whether you are still thinking about how to start or are working with your small group, creative ways to capture some of God's vision for a group of churches can be extremely helpful. One way I have seen work well is the following simple exercise.

You ask the group to pretend that a church friend of theirs has just moved away. Then ask them to imagine that three years go past. They have, therefore, arrived at a date three years into the future, when the churches have made real progress in a number of areas. Ask people, working entirely on their own, to write a letter to that friend from the perspective of this new future date, telling them what the churches in this group are like now. Ask them to describe what has happened in the last three years to bring them to this good place in the present.

For this exercise to work well, you may need to explain it more than once for people to get the idea. Once they have, pray for inspiration, then allow a decent amount of time for letter writing. You may prefer that people go away and work on it, then bring it back to a subsequent gathering.

Whichever way you do it, the exercise allows people to think with prayerful creativity about what matters most to them about their group of churches, including their deepest desires for them. It also relieves them of thinking about all the possible problems that could arise to derail their dreams because, in this exercise, they have already happened.

Once the letters are written, move on to the second, possibly more challenging, part of the exercise. Ask each person to read out their letter in turn and see where the common threads are, where the imaginative things are that people seem inspired by, and where the Spirit of God seems to be at work. This exercise will bring joy and delight as you rejoice in a possible future untrammelled by people's anxieties over money, energy and resources. Or even by that dreaded phrase: 'We tried it before and it didn't work.'

The third and most practical part of the exercise might take some weeks or months. Taking the agreed things from this looking-back-from-the-future work, plus any wider vision statements you have looked at, you hone them.

Some ideas will need to be abandoned, others refined. You are aiming for a vision that is robust, compelling and straightforward enough for people across the churches to embrace with enthusiasm. Then they will be willing to work and pray for it. With enough grace and humour, we have so much we can give to and learn from each other.

Putting vision into practice

Having grown in confidence in putting short-term plans into effect, it should now be possible for your small group to take this longer-term vision and start working on it across your MPB. As anyone who has done this before knows, the vision needs to be divided into manageable steps, with some 'quick wins' early on to create momentum.

You will need the small group of people to continue to meet regularly and pray committedly to keep the plans moving on, and there also has to be willingness to make adjustments, or even big changes, as situations alter or there are personnel changes. As we noted in the last chapter, consistent, good communication and open flexibility to the leading of God into new things will keep people informed and invested in the progress.

You cannot lose

What is there to lose by dreaming of a vision? While it could feel alarming to tie our colours to the mast or to consider the possibility of failing to achieve the vision, if we do not even try we might find ourselves stagnating or losing ground. Many of us may well be anxious about the credibility of our own leadership or that of the action team if things go wrong, especially if we anticipate opposition or conflict.

However, ultimately the identity of all of us as church leaders is in Christ and what he has done – it is not in what we achieve or get wrong (Romans 5.1–11). We would do well to remind ourselves that God's love for us is committed and faithful whatever we do, good or bad. We are always sinners saved by grace. We can, therefore, risk the dreams and visions that the Spirit gives because, succeed or fail, we are safe in God's love.

We can also be confident in the fact that God loves our churches, and the communities they serve, far more than we ever can. His purposes are good and he will answer us when we seek his kingdom. 'Your kingdom come. Your will be done' (Matthew 6.10) is one of the most powerful prayers we can pray. We may just rattle through the words but if we allow it to go deep inside us instead, as a constant part of our praying, we make room for God to open up his ways ahead.

It is all about hope

One of the best things about facilitating the CPAS learning communities has been seeing MPBs gaining in hope. Often, hard-working, prayerful, committed people arrive at the first session rather weary and discouraged. Yet being together with others, learning together, worshipping and praying together, encouraging each other and sharing ideas seem to bring new hope. As short-term plans are put into effect and longer-range dreams and visions start to emerge, there is a renewed energy for what God wants to do among them. Hope rises again.

And with hope, people can commit to new things, let go of old ways of doing things that may have outlived their usefulness, breathe new life into spiritual practices and take risks to bring in a better future. In the process they can also get to know each other better, have lots of fun, share the disappointments, recalibrate the plans together and rejoice in belonging to the family of God.

In your discerning, shaping and sharing of vision, then, you are creating a higher level of hope. And hope will continue to rise as people see the vision coming into being over several years, even when there are some setbacks along the way.

Keeping momentum

It is, therefore, important that we as leaders are positive in our outlook and take care to keep momentum going. There are four practices that will help with that:

1 Have an attitude of continual encouragement. Be like Barnabas in the New Testament, whose name, a nickname, means 'son of encouragement' (Acts 4.36). Look for all the ways you can give words of encouragement. They must be sincere words because flattery is easily discerned and quickly dismissed. It also undermines trust. Give genuine and proportionate praise wherever and whenever you can.
2 Publicly celebrate every milestone, big and small. Telling the stories of change, growth and achievement in as many creative ways as you can keeps people engaged and enthused. Tell the stories in print, on internet platforms, through interviews and video clips, photos and posters. Occasional gatherings across the whole benefice to celebrate progress have great positive effect.
3 Own up to mistakes or problems quickly and take responsibility for them, assuring people you will regroup and reset. Being honest about things that go wrong, and not blaming others, ensures that people will continue being willing to take risks.
4 Say thank you, publicly and often, for the things that people do. Thank them on behalf of the whole MPB. Send thank-you notes from the action team. Thank people privately if they seriously do not want to be in the spotlight.

Stay flexible

If we are committed to prayer and seeking God as we work on a vision together, we will also see the need to remain flexible in all that we do. Consider this quote:

> Carefully planned strategies will only get us so far in understanding God's way forward. This is not to diminish their importance in any way. Christian leaders have a God given responsibility to use their power of reason, imagination and intellect. But the experience

of God's people again and again has been that it is God's surprises rather than their own plans that open up the future in remarkable ways ... God is a God of life and growth, and growth is irregular and unpredictable, but also irrepressible and thrillingly beautiful. If things point in one direction, but God seems to be leading somewhere else, our advice is go for God every time.

(Mike Booker and Mark Ireland, *Evangelism – which way now?*, London: Church House Publishing, 2003, p. 188)

If we are serious in following God's good plans and ideas for our churches, then we will be wise to be open to the new things he does and the new ways he leads us.

All of this, as we will have found out repeatedly by now, requires us to be courageous and persistent. The early disciples in Acts had to be courageous, prayerful, strategic and flexible as they sought to bring the gospel to 'Jerusalem, in all Judea and Samaria, and to the ends of the earth' (Acts 1.8). Just like them, we need those characteristics to mark our work across our churches.

Questions to consider

1 Do you need a longer-range vision at this stage in your journey as a benefice? Has your own experience of discerning a vision in different settings been largely positive or discouraging?

2 What do you think of any of the multiple visions – from the national church, diocese, deanery or mission area – there are in your situation? How do you see your churches relating to them?

3 If you decide to work towards each church having its own vision as part of a benefice vision, spend time reflecting on each church community. What might God be calling the people there to concentrate on, and what might they offer to the rest of the group?

4 How confident are you about your action team putting vision into practice? How can you all inspire each other to get going and keep going? How can you keep stoking the fires of hope?

5 How can you adopt the practices for momentum that you are not already following? Who could you thank today? What sort of storytelling event could you plan? How can you inject life into these ideas and make it all more fun and memorable?

Story time

One vicar and her action team in a learning community had several churches needing building work all at once. Working with others, they made a plan that would see all the work done in turn on the buildings, and they obtained both local and national grants to help it happen. However, the vision for the work was not about buildings as such, but rather about growing the churches, blessing the people and helping them do mission well. Alongside the building work they planted a new informal family church and committed to helping people walk in their faith more deeply. The work on the buildings certainly took up time and energy but also enabled more links with the community and opened up opportunities for outreach. This action team had a clear vision and a workable plan. They put it into effect and they rejoiced in seeing many levels of growth.

13

And Finally

What now?

The final question, then, having got to this point in the book, is: 'What are you going to do as a result of reading it?'

Do go back to the Introduction and read again about the other three interlocking resources that accompany this book and decide if you want to use them.

May God bless you as you journey on with your churches through all the joys and challenges of working in a multi-parish benefice.

Resources

Chapter 1 The Star – Looking at how things are now

Thrive collection of resources: *Thrive: Helping Your Multi-parish Benefice to Grow* (book), *Thrive Prayer Guide* (booklet), Thrive course (download), Thrive PCC sessions (download), all available from www.cpas.org.uk.

Chapter 2 Our Praying – Finding the foundational place

Lectio 365 app and website: https://www.24-7prayer.com/resource/lectio-365.

Thy Kingdom Come app and website: https://www.thykingdomcome.global.

Stephen Cottrell, *Prayer: Where to start and how to keep going*, London: Church House Publishing, 2020.

Pete Greig, *How to Pray: A simple guide for normal people*, London: Hodder & Stoughton, 2019.

Pete Greig, The Prayer Course, https://prayercourse.org.

Chapter 3 Our Stories, Part 1 – Mapping our stories, past, present and future

Rebuilders app and website: https://rebuilders.co/home.

Chapter 4 Our Stories, Part 2 – Relating well across the group

Thrive PCC sessions (download), https://www.cpas.org.uk.

Avery Dulles, *Models of Church*, New York: Image, 2002.

Bob Jackson, *What Makes Churches Grow? Vision and practice in effective mission*, London: Church House Publishing, 2015.

Chapter 5 Our Leaders, Part 1 – Rediscovering the body of Christ

James Lawrence, *Growing Leaders*, Abingdon: Bible Reading Fellowship, 2020 and course (CPAS download).

Ruth Hassell, *Growing Young Leaders*, Abingdon: Bible Reading Fellowship, 2022 and course (CPAS download).

Dr Ian Jagelman, *The Empowered Church: Releasing ministry through effective leadership*, Port Orchard, WA: Ark House Press, 2016.

Chapter 6 Our Leaders, Part 2 – Growing great teams

Patrick Lencioni, *The Five Dysfunctions of a Team*, San Francisco, CA: Jossey-Bass, 2002.

James Lawrence, *Leading Well with Others*, Grove Leadership Series L40, Cambridge: Grove Books, www.cpas.org.uk.

Chapter 7 Our Disciples, Part 1 – Being disciples

Tracy Cotterell, Neil Hudson, *Leading a Whole-life Disciplemaking Church*, Grove Leadership Series L7, Cambridge: Grove Books, www.cpas.org.uk.

London Institute for Contemporary Christianity, https://licc.org.uk, a range of resources for everyday discipleship.

Dallas Willard, *The Divine Conspiracy*, London: William Collins, 2014.

Chapter 8 Our Disciples, Part 2 – Becoming lifelong disciples together

John Mark Comer, *The Ruthless Elimination of Hurry*, London: Hodder & Stoughton, 2019.

Lucy Peppiatt, *The Disciple: On becoming truly human*, Eugene, OR: Cascade Books, 2012.

Andy Frost and Katharine Hill, *Raising Faith: Helping our children find a faith that lasts*, Cardiff: Care For The Family, 2018.

Parenting for Faith resources available from https://www.parentingforfaith.brf.org.uk.

Chapter 9 Our Faith Sharing, Part 1 – Learning and practising

James Lawrence, *How to Nurture a Faith-sharing Culture: Creative ideas to inspire church leaders*, Coventry: CPAS, 2022.
Thrive PCC sessions (download), www.cpas.org.uk.

Chapter 10 Our Faith Sharing, Part 2 – Events and involvement

Stephen Cottrell, *From the Abundance of the Heart*, London: Darton, Longman & Todd, 2006.
Bob Jackson and George Fisher, *Everybody Welcome*, London: Church House Publishing, 2011.

Chapter 11 Our Future, Part 1 – Assessing and prioritizing

Michael Hyatt, *No-Fail Communication: 13 Workplace Communication Problems and How to Fix Them*, Franklin, TN: Michael Hyatt and Company, 2020.
Alastair McKay, *Bridgebuilding*, London: Canterbury Press, 2019.

Chapter 12 Our Future, Part 2 – Working on vision

Robert Atwell, Gill Ambrose and Helen Bent, *How Village Churches Thrive*, London: Church House Publishing, 2022.
Mark Ireland and Mike Chew, *How to Do Mission Action Planning*, London: SPCK, 2009.

About CPAS

CPAS enables churches to help every person in the UK and Republic of Ireland hear and discover the good news of Jesus Christ.

Local church mission is the heartbeat of CPAS. As an Anglican evangelical mission agency, we believe that the good news about Jesus is real and relevant to all people and that effective local church ministry is key to seeing women, men, young people and children come to faith in Christ.

We make mission possible by developing Christian leaders through leadership training, equipping churches with much-needed resources to help them grow, running Venture and Falcon holidays and School Ventures for thousands of 8–18-year-olds each year, and appointing mission-minded clergy through our patronage work with just under 700 churches.

To find out more, go to: www.cpas.org.uk. Facebook, Twitter, Instagram, YouTube @CPASNews.